Managing change

MANCHESTER
UNIVERSITY PRESS

Managing change

A guide to British economic policy

Graham Ingham

Manchester University Press

Manchester and New York

distributed exclusively in the USA by St. Martin's Press

Copyright © Graham Ingham 2000

The right of Graham Ingham to be identified as the author of this work has been asserted by him in accordance with the Copyright, Designs and Patents Act 1988.

Published by Manchester University Press
Oxford Road, Manchester M13 9NR, UK
and Room 400, 175 Fifth Avenue, New York, NY 10010, USA
http://www.man.ac.uk/mup

Distributed exclusively in the USA by
St. Martin's Press, Inc., 175 Fifth Avenue, New York,
NY 10010, USA

Distributed exclusively in Canada by
UBC Press, University of British Columbia, 2029 West Mall,
Vancouver, BC, Canada V6T 1Z2

British Library Cataloguing-in-Publication Data
A catalogue record for this book is available from the British Library

Library of Congress Cataloging-in-Publication Data
Ingham, Graham.
   Managing change: a guide to British economic policy / Graham Ingham.
      p. cm.
   Includes index.
   ISBN 0-7190-5764-7 – ISBN 0-7190-5765-5 (pbk.)
      1. Great Britain–Economic policy–1997. 2. Fiscal policy–Great Britain. 3. Industrial policy–Great Britain. I. Title.
   HC256.7.I54 2000
   338.941–dc21

                                                                  00-022265

ISBN   0 7190 5764 7   *hardback*
       0 7190 5765 5   *paperback*

First published 2000

07 06 05 04 03 02 01 00   10 9 8 7 6 5 4 3 2 1

Typeset by Ralph Footring, Derby
Printed in Great Britain by Bell & Bain Ltd, Glasgow

Contents

Boxes, tables and figures

Boxes

Tables

Figure

Preface

On most Saturday evenings, the streets of central London – especially those around Covent Garden and Trafalgar Square, the heart of London's theatre land – are full of people out for a good time, off to the theatre or the cinema or a restaurant or a pub. But anyone who happened to be there on Saturday, 31 March 1990, would have been both shocked and afraid. Even the television news pictures, broadcast around the world, were alarming. Burning cars and broken glass littered the streets; rioting mobs replaced the Saturday night crowds. Mounted police in full riot gear were everywhere. Four hundred police officers were injured and 339 people arrested. It looked like a city in the throes of a revolution.

But the rioting that weekend was not in protest against political oppression. It was an uprising sparked off by economic policy – specifically the poll tax, or community charge – which had been introduced in Scotland the previous year and was to be introduced in England and Wales the following day. The poll tax was the replacement for the rates – local property taxes which provided much of the money spent on schools, housing and street cleaning services by local authorities. The rioters did not succeed in persuading the government of Prime Minister Margaret Thatcher to alter its plans: the poll tax went ahead as planned. But within eight months Thatcher had been replaced as Prime Minister. The deep unpopularity of the poll tax was an important factor in the Conservatives' decision to find a new leader. And the tax itself was replaced in 1993.

Economic policy rarely generates quite such an extreme reaction as the poll tax riots. But it is something about which we all hold opinions, no matter how strongly or gently we choose to express them. Economic policy is something that affects all of us directly, every day, from the day we are born to the day we are buried or cremated. It affects how much we earn, whether we have a job, how much we pay in taxes, the prices of the goods and services we buy, the rate we in Britain get when converting pounds into other currencies when we go on a foreign holiday or business trip. Our education and that of our children; the sort of health care we get if we are sick; the state of the train services and the roads; whether we have access to a bus service; how much we have to pay for theatre tickets: these are all aspects of our lives on which economic policy-makers have some impact.

That is not to say that economic policy-makers sit down and decide each of those things. Of course, if the Chancellor raises the duty on cigarettes or petrol, he is directly determining their extra cost. But, in most cases, the impact of economic policy is far more complicated, the link between what policy-makers do and how it affects each of us far more obscure and uncertain.

How public policy is formulated depends on several factors: the traditional structure of the policy-making framework, which in Britain's case has gradually developed over more than two centuries; the international environment, which is of increasing importance to policy-makers; changing domestic circumstances; the political climate; and the climate of ideas. To look at how policy is made today we need to know fairly obvious things like who does what; who is able to influence whom, and how. We also need to know how changing ideas have affected and do affect policy and policy-making.

That is what this book is about. It is a lot to pack into a short volume. This is therefore a modest book, with immodest aims. The intention is to give the reader a general understanding of how economic policy is made in Britain. It tries not to assume too much previous knowledge of economics: you will not find any econometric equations here, and no more numbers than needed to clarify points in the text. It also assumes relatively little historical knowledge although, despite what some people believe, policy cannot be made in a vacuum, without any sense of what has gone before. The history of exchange rate policy, for instance, is littered with examples of policy-makers repeating the mistakes of their predecessors. Governments find it politically difficult to abandon defence of a particular exchange rate even when the economic arguments for change are compelling. I make no apology, therefore, for the historical content of this book, nor for its starting point: 1945, besides being the end of the Second World War, marked a major turning point in economic policy in the industrialised world. Much of what was introduced then has since become unfashionable or discredited: it is important to understand how and why.

In some cases, the circumstances of the moment may leave policy-makers with no alternative but to stick with a policy they suspect or know to be wrong. It is easy to criticise from the outside or with hindsight. But policy-makers, and in particular politicians, are fond of convincing themselves that the world has fundamentally changed – often because of policies for which they are responsible – and that therefore the past has little to teach them. Of course, there are changes which fundamentally alter longstanding economic relationships. But looked at over a very long period, these tend to be fewer than you might think. The evidence clearly suggests, for instance, that for more than a hundred years Britain has grappled with some remarkably similar economic problems: poor productivity growth, a poor education and training record and, all too often, an overvalued exchange rate. Being able to distinguish between structural and cyclical factors remains one of the biggest challenges for economic policy-makers. Politicians have frequently come to regret grandiose claims about the transformation of the British economy, because they subsequently discovered they were actually speaking just as the downturn started.

But we should not be too hard on the politicians. Yes, they do sometimes make such claims for political reasons, to boost their electoral standing. But their mistaken rhetoric can simply reflect the difficulty of knowing what is happening to the economy at any given point. Some policy decisions – perhaps most – cannot wait until all the necessary facts are available. They require a judgement to be made on the usually incomplete evidence available at the time. Economists are often reluctant to admit it, but economic forecasting remains an imprecise art.

This book sets out to illuminate some of the problems which policy-makers face, and to give some sense of the constraints within which they have to operate and of the process by which economic policy is made. Each chapter is, as far as possible, self-contained. That occasionally calls for repetition of some points and some cross-references to other chapters: these have been kept to a minimum.

The book broadly divides into three parts: Chapters 1 and 2 set policy in context, both international and historical; Chapters 3 and 4 focus on the process of policy-making itself, both domestically and in the context of British membership of the European Union; and Chapters 5–10 look at specific policy areas. This cannot claim to be a comprehensive account of all policy: space does not permit that. But anyone reading the book as a whole should have a much clearer sense of the issues that affect policy-making and the main areas of policy.

There will be those who object to the extent to which the book focuses on government: in an era of globalisation, they will argue, governments are not the only important actors in the economy. Indeed, it has been argued in some quarters that governments have relatively little freedom of manoeuvre in a modern industrial economy and that to focus on government policy-making is therefore a mistake. I do not accept that argument. It is true that governments find themselves subject to greater constraints than in the past. The financial markets, for example, can have a much greater and more immediate impact than they did even twenty or thirty years ago. Multinational companies can also bring greater pressure to bear on governments than they used to, partly because they now have far more freedom to determine the location of their headquarters and their main functions. But these are matters of degree. Much of eighteenth- and nineteenth-century economic policy was influenced by business interests as well: one has only to think of the East India and Hudson's Bay companies or the imperialist expansion of the Victorian era to realise that. And financial markets have been playing their part in government policy for more than two centuries – the South Sea Bubble of 1720 and the abandonment of the Gold Standard in 1931 are just two examples.

I have tried to reflect the new and different pressures on public policy-makers in examining the policy process and in the thematic chapters. It may be that the accelerating development of communications and other technology, and in particular the spectacular growth of Internet use and e-commerce, will fundamentally change the role of government in many areas of economic policy. But at the time of writing, their impact has not, in my view, changed the central role which public policy plays in issues such as employment, inflation and monetary policy, though it has, in many instances, imposed greater constraints on policy-making and made it considerably more difficult.

This is not a book about ideas or economic theory. A survey of the changes in economics in the past fifty years would be a formidable task and beyond the scope of this book. What I have aimed to do, as far as possible, is show how ideas can form one element of the policy-making process: how John Maynard Keynes, for instance, influenced the policy-makers of the post-war period, or the impact which Milton Friedman and others had on monetary policy in the late 1970s and after. At least as important as understanding the relevance of these ideas, however, is an understanding of their limitations in a policy-making environment. The real world is fundamentally different from an economic model, and usually in ways we cannot anticipate or even fully understand. The policy-maker has to judge how far a theory might work in this real world and how far it is impracticable. It may be impracticable for reasons unrelated to economics, of course. The policy adopted at any given juncture may depend far more on the individuals involved or the political constraints on policy-makers.

Economic policy is not the result of a systematic scientific process. As much rigour as possible should be incorporated into the formulation of policy. That should at least reduce the number of nasty surprises in store when something does not go according to plan. But it will not eliminate nasty surprises, as every experienced policy-maker knows. And nothing ever goes exactly according to plan. This book is above all an attempt to explain, in the British context, why this is so, and to give some understanding of the many factors which ensure that this is perhaps the only certain rule in the making of economic policy.

October 1999

Acknowledgements

Several people played a crucial role in the production of this book. Margaret Doxey provided help and encouragement at exactly the right moments and took the trouble to read and comment on a late draft. Jonathan Birt read the work in draft more than once, provided helpful comments and generally put up with more than anyone should have to during the book's gestation. Sue Holloway came to my rescue by giving me helpful guidance on figures. Mary Yacoob has provided much-needed secretarial assistance. Nicola Viinikka was an understanding and patient editor whose encouragement I greatly appreciated; likewise, her assistant, Pippa Kenyon, was unfailingly helpful. Ralph Footring was an impressively thorough and helpful copy-editor.

But above all I want to acknowledge the help of the late Susan Strange, my friend and generous mentor for so many years, and who made one final contribution to our friendship and my career. She was responsible for introducing me to Nicola Viinikka. Without Susan this book would therefore never have been written and it is dedicated to her memory.

Abbreviations

CAP	Common Agricultural Policy
DEA	Department of Economic Affairs
DfEE	Department for Education and Employment
ECSC	European Coal and Steel Community
EEC	European Economic Community
EFTA	European Free Trade Association
EIB	European Investment Bank
EMS	European Monetary System
EMU	Economic and Monetary Union
ERM	Exchange Rate Mechanism
EU	European Union
Euratom	European Atomic Energy Community
FCO	Foreign and Commonwealth Office
GDP	gross domestic product
IBRD	International Bank for Reconstruction and Development
ILO	International Labour Organisation
IMF	International Monetary Fund
MPC	Monetary Policy Committee
MTFS	Medium-Term Financial Strategy
NAIRU	non-accelerating inflation rate of unemployment
NEB	National Enterprise Board
NHS	National Health Service
NMW	national minimum wage
OECD	Organisation for Economic Co-operation and Development
OPEC	Organisation of Petroleum Exporting Countries
PFI	Private Finance Initiative
QMV	qualified majority voting
SERPS	State Earnings Related Pension Scheme
TUC	Trades Union Congress
VAT	value-added tax

1   The international context

The world economy in 1945

By 1945, six years of war had had a significant impact on every industrial nation. Many developing countries had also been deeply affected. The effects of war were military, political, physical and, of course, economic in nature. They had all, in some way, influenced the shape of the global economy which policy-makers in Britain and around the world confronted as the war drew to an end.

The most obvious change was the physical destruction in many countries: pretty much the whole of Europe, Japan and former European colonies in North Africa, the Middle East and the Far East had suffered to some degree. In Germany and Japan, and in parts of Eastern Europe, the loss of physical capital was huge. There was extreme material deprivation and starvation in some parts of Europe, which had to be dealt with as quickly as possible. Many countries had had their economies totally dominated by the war effort. Around two-thirds of UK gross domestic product (GDP) was taken up with war-related economic activity by 1945. Even in the US, which had largely escaped physical damage, the war effort had been considerable. Other countries, such as France, Italy and the Netherlands, along with several British colonial outposts in the Far East, had been under occupation, often for several years.

These, then, were the main changes. Policy-makers needed to respond to them and some of their less visible consequences. At first sight, it might appear that the post-war world was divided between victors and the vanquished, but the truth was more complicated. It is true that Germany and Japan, for instance, had been defeated on every level. It is also true that the US and the UK were the principal military victors (along with the USSR). But in economic terms Britain was closer to Germany than the US. For the UK, the war had been fought

1

at enormous cost: external supplies for the war had cost £10,000 million – roughly double national income in 1945. Half of this money had come from the US under the lend–lease arrangements: in theory, this money had to be repaid once the war was over. In the end, Britain had to find only about £650 million of this. But by 1945 the country's finances were in dire straits. Britain was once more looking to the US for help. America had benefited substantially in economic terms from participation in the war. The US war effort – government-funded economic activity on a massive scale – ensured that the country finally escaped from the Great Depression. The US economy's ability to deliver weaponry for its allies boosted economic growth.

This combination of a dramatic decline in British economic power and the consolidation of US wealth was crucial in determining the shape of the post-war global economy. The US had outstripped Britain in economic size and wealth since before the end of the nineteenth century. But as late as 1914 Britain remained the world's largest exporter of capital and the lynchpin of the Gold Standard system (which by making national currencies ultimately convertible into gold determined their value relative to each other). But Britain's economic power was rapidly eroded during the First World War and the inter-war period: the Second World War accelerated and confirmed the decline which was already taking place. The US dollar had dominated the Gold Standard system – which Britain abandoned in 1931 – throughout the inter-war period. British political and economic influence no longer derived from real economic power, although Britain's central role in the war tended to encourage the political class to overlook this fact. By 1945 America called the shots.

A new world economic order

The extent of these fundamental changes, and their implications, had begun to emerge even before the war had ended. Preparations for a new post-war economic structure had begun in earnest in July 1944, when the Americans and the British convened the Bretton Woods Conference (so-called because it was held at Bretton Woods, New Hampshire). The aims of those at the Conference were simple but ambitious. They wanted to put in place new mechanisms for organising the world economy. They also wanted to avoid the costly mistakes made in the aftermath of the First World War (when the scale of war

reparations enforced on Germany were widely thought to have contributed to the rise of Hitler). And they intended to eliminate the
destructive approach to economic policy seen in the 1930s, when
countries had damagingly pursued protectionist trade policies and
imposed high tariffs on imports. All this, of course, ran in parallel with
plans for new *political* structures, in particular the United Nations.

The Bretton Woods Conference established a new international
monetary system for currencies (see Box 8.2 on page 157). Once
currencies were fixed (initially at the rates obtaining in July 1944) they
could vary only by plus or minus 1 per cent and be changed only under
exceptional circumstances. This was known as a fixed but adjustable
peg system. The Gold Standard had been abandoned, but US dollars
could still be exchanged for gold at the fixed price of $35 per ounce.
For those countries with temporary balance-of-payments difficulties,
which might in other circumstances have prompted a devaluation, new
borrowing facilities were provided to avoid a change in the exchange
rate. At the same time, the new system was meant to ensure an adequate
supply of capital in the world, to finance investment. The aim was to
create a three-pronged approach to international economic management by creating three new international institutions:

1 the International Monetary Fund (IMF), whose job would be to
   supervise the new international monetary system, to help member
   countries with short-term balance-of-payments problems and to
   ensure that there was enough *liquidity* in the system – in other
   words to make sure there was enough international capital available
   to fund investment;
2 the International Bank for Reconstruction and Development (IBRD)
   (which became known as the World Bank), which would be able to
   lend money to countries in need of physical reconstruction;
3 the World Trade Organisation, to regulate world trade and to promote freer trade by reducing both tariff and non-tariff barriers.

This last did not finally come into being until 1995: the US Congress
refused to ratify the original proposals in 1945. In 1948, the General
Agreement on Tariffs and Trade (GATT) was established, but this was
a weak substitute, a framework for trade liberalisation rather than an
institution with teeth of its own. Nevertheless, the commitment in
principle to the concept of free trade marked the end of Britain's
Imperial Preference system (which aimed to give preferential treatment

to goods traded within the British Empire), heavily criticised by the US in the 1930s.

Proof that the US was now the dominant global power came during the Bretton Woods negotiations. John Maynard Keynes, the leading British negotiator, had very clear ideas about the system he wanted. So too did the US chief negotiator, Harry Dexter White. Where the two men's ideas differed, White's view prevailed.

A bipolar economic world

The other big change in the post-war world was the emergence of the Eastern bloc – the greatly enlarged Soviet empire. Russia had pursued an autarkic economic policy since the 1917 Revolution. But during the course of the Second World War, the Soviet leader, Josef Stalin, had seized the opportunity greatly to extend the sphere of Russian influence and control. Negotiations between the US, Britain and the USSR at Yalta and Potsdam essentially gave the USSR control over most of Central and Eastern Europe, including East Germany, Poland, Hungary, Czechoslovakia and Bulgaria. From 1945, the world economy was therefore divided into two: the West, dominated by the US, and the Soviet empire under Stalin, with relatively little exchange between the two. In a speech in Fulton, Missouri, in 1946, Churchill famously described this breakdown in relations between the former wartime allies when he said 'from Stettin in the Baltic to Trieste in the Adriatic an iron curtain has descended across the Continent'.

The extent of this gap was illustrated in 1947 when the US plan for Marshall aid – the European Recovery Program – was announced. The countries of Western Europe, all struggling to recover from the impact of war, were grateful for American help. The aid programme, conceived by the US Secretary of State, George Marshall, was not given for solely philanthropic reasons: the Americans were anxious to establish a European bulwark against Stalin's empire. But the amounts on offer were nevertheless remarkably generous – equivalent in Britain's case to around 5.5 per cent of GDP in 1949 (and proportionately much greater amounts for some countries such as the Netherlands). Stalin refused to participate, even though the offer of aid was, in theory, open to all countries in Europe.

Britain's new world role

This was the world which Britain's economic policy-makers faced as the country emerged from the war militarily victorious but economically much weaker than anyone realised or understood at the time. This misunderstanding partly arose because of the devastating impact the war had had on the major continental European economies, particularly France and Germany. Britain still seemed to be in a stronger position. In 1950, for example, British GDP per capita was higher than that of France or Germany. But for decades before the war the British economy had been declining in relative terms. Growth in GDP and in productivity had been slow by international comparisons – British productivity growth was half that of the US during the 1930s, for example. Britain's share of world trade and world manufacturing output had been falling for many years. What appeared to be a recovery immediately after the war mainly reflected the extremely weak position of other countries (the UK's share of world manufacturing exports grew from 21 per cent in 1937 to 24 per cent in 1950). The consistently superior performance of these countries after about 1950 (see Table 1.1) was the principal source of many of Britain's subsequent difficulties.

It is important to remember both that Britain's post-war economic decline was relative and that it was not new. Britain had been the first country to industrialise. Its dominant position in the world economy in the nineteenth century was bound to be challenged as other countries began to catch up. The UK had historically experienced much lower

Table 1.1 Comparative economic performance, 1950–73

	GDP per capita (average annual compound rate)	Unemployment as % of the labour force	Change in consumer price index	Productivity growth (average annual compound rate)
France	4.0	2.0	5.0	5.1
Germany	5.0	2.5	2.7	6.0
UK	2.5	2.8	4.6	3.1
US	2.4	4.6	2.7	2.7

From Angus Maddison, *Monitoring the world economy 1820–1992* (OECD, 1995).

long-term growth rates than many of its competitors and the post-war experience in some respects was simply a continuation of this. Economic historians have argued over the extent to which this decline was inevitable – Britain's poor productivity record is partly attributed to the failure of industry to appreciate the importance of capital investment. But Britain's post-war performance is widely accepted to have been unnecessarily bad. It left policy-makers with the challenge of managing this decline and, in the later part of the twentieth century, trying to reverse it.

The philosophical context

In July 1945, with the war against Germany over, but the war with Japan still not concluded, Britain's new Labour government came to power after an unexpected landslide election victory. This government, which replaced the wartime coalition administration led by the Conservative leader, Churchill, had a clear economic agenda: the creation of a national health service, radical changes in welfare and educational provision, and a commitment to state ownership of the means of production. Such policies marked a radical departure from the pre-war management of the economy. But by 1945 they were not so far removed from the economic policies of the Conservative opposition: indeed, some of these policies, such as those on education and employment, had already been espoused by the coalition government (of which Labour had been a member). Even more significantly, such an interventionist approach had much in common with the economic philosophy prevailing elsewhere in the industrial world. By 1945 a much broader consensus about the role of the public sector in the world economy was apparent. President Franklin Roosevelt's New Deal policies in the US, Keynes's *General Theory* – which led politicians to believe full employment was an attainable objective – and the war itself had all contributed to a belief that government had an important part to play not just in the provision of public services but in regulating demand in the economy. Keynes's point was that when demand collapsed, as it had in the 1930s, government could – and should – play a critical role in stimulating it (see Box 1.1).

The state's role in alleviating unemployment was also enhanced, both by the events of the 1930s and by the war. Politicians recognised that they had a responsibility and an obligation to provide jobs for the

Box 1.1 John Maynard Keynes

John Maynard Keynes (1883–1946) was probably the most influential economist of the twentieth century. His theories dominated economic thinking for decades. Keynes had been a Treasury official as well as an academic and he wrote a number of influential works, including a critique of the peace terms agreed at the end of the First World War. He was a key figure in the wartime Bretton Woods negotiations, which established the post-war international economic settlement; and he led the British team which negotiated the huge loan from the US in 1945.

But it was Keynes's *General Theory of Employment, Interest and Money* (published in 1936) which had the most far-reaching and long-lasting influence and which gave birth to the economic approach known as Keynesianism. Essentially, Keynes argued that supply and demand in the economy could be balanced irrespective of whether everyone had a job. There were, he said, many points of balance, or equilibrium, not all of which provided for full employment. Keynes argued that it was up to the government to make sure that the level of demand in the economy was sufficiently high to deliver full employment.

This revolutionised contemporary economic thinking, which had hitherto assumed that the high unemployment levels of the 1930s were an aberration from the norm. Keynes's views led governments to intervene much more actively in the economy to try to manage the level of demand – with often unsatisfactory results.

millions of men whose military service was now ending. Public works programmes, and governments' own demand for goods and services, could create jobs and so reduce unemployment.

The golden age

Recovery from the effects of war came more quickly than predicted, partly because of the widespread willingness of governments to take a more active, interventionist role than hitherto. By the early 1950s, the industrial world was, by and large, enjoying unprecedented levels of economic growth. In hindsight, this appears to have been a golden age for the industrial world. GDP grew rapidly in most industrial countries. Inflation was low: not particularly so by the standards of the pre-1939 world, but certainly compared with anything which would be experienced in the 1970s and 1980s. Unemployment, too, was remarkably low: for most of the 1950s and 1960s, in most industrial countries, it was not a major political problem – even though governments had at least implicitly accepted a commitment to full employment, however vaguely defined, as a political obligation. In the US, Western Europe and Japan productivity growth was remarkable by the standards of anything which had been seen since the Industrial Revolution.

Dramatic economic improvements in the Western world after 1945 were matched by the momentum for closer economic ties among these countries. The creation of the Bretton Woods institutions reflected in part the belief that international economic co-operation could lessen the risk of military confrontation in the future. This belief drove the key political figures in Europe to argue that ever-closer co-operation was the key to averting war, especially between West Germany and its neighbours. Strengthen the economies ties between these countries, it was argued, and conflict would become unthinkable. The first concrete proposal came in 1950, for a European Coal and Steel Community (ECSC) aimed at co-ordinating coal and steel production across Western Europe: at that time, these were key factors of production.

Britain and international co-operation

It was at this point that the UK began to diverge significantly from its European neighbours. Six countries initially signed up for membership of the ECSC: Belgium, France, Luxembourg, Italy, the Netherlands and West Germany. The UK was invited, even urged to join: but although they kept a close watch on developments and the subsequent moves towards closer economic integration, the policy-makers of both main political parties remained aloof. They continued to do so when the European Economic Community (EEC) was set up by the Treaty of Rome in 1957 (it started life in 1958). Instead, the UK was a driving force behind what might be termed the multilateral as opposed to the integrationist approach. A commitment to free trade, coupled with concern at developments among 'the Six', led to the creation of the European Free Trade Association (EFTA) in May 1960, initially comprising, in addition to Britain, Austria, Denmark, Norway, Portugal, Sweden and Switzerland.

The following year saw the establishment of the Organisation for Economic Co-operation and Development (OECD). This was the successor to the Organisation for European Economic Co-operation set up in 1948 to administer the Marshall aid programme. The OECD was larger and also included the US and Canada as members; Japan joined in 1964, and Mexico and South Korea became members more recently. The OECD has no real powers. But from its inception it has provided another forum for the open discussion of economic problems, and added another resource for economic surveillance to those developing in Washington with the IMF and the IBRD.

These attempts at economic co-operation, however, often masked reality. The international monetary system established at Bretton Woods was plagued by problems from its inception. The idea of a fixed but adjustable peg system of exchange rates, backed up with IMF help for countries needing to adjust, was intended to prevent a repetition of the competitive devaluations which had occurred in the 1930s. But strain in the new system was evident from the beginning, and only to be expected as recovery from war got under way. The UK was forced to devalue sterling from £1 = \$4.03 to £1 = \$2.80 in 1949. By the early 1960s, tensions in the system were again beginning to mount up. Britain was, in a sense, at the centre of these problems: the value of the pound was frequently under pressure in the foreign exchange markets.

Sterling was not alone, of course. As the big industrial economies grew rapidly in the period of post-war recovery, they did so at different rates of growth of GDP, productivity and inflation. Even small differences could, over time, become significant and they did, making the existing structure of exchange rates increasingly inappropriate. The German mark, for instance, was under almost constant *upward* pressure during the 1960s, while sterling was being pushed in the opposite direction. But these problems were compounded by the great reluctance of those concerned to make any changes to existing exchange rates, in spite of the fact that the system was meant to be adjustable.

The collapse of Bretton Woods

The second enforced devaluation of sterling, in 1967 (see Chapter 2), was, as many had rightly feared, the beginning of the end for the Bretton Woods system. After sterling gave way there was pressure on the price of gold. As a result, from March 1968 there were two prices for gold – the \$35 per ounce at which central banks could trade gold between themselves and a much higher, fluctuating market price for others who wanted to trade in the precious metal. Coinciding with these systemic disturbances was the decision of the US government to finance the burgeoning costs of its involvement in the Vietnam War by borrowing. By the late 1960s Vietnam, together with President Lyndon Johnson's hugely expensive Great Society programme of welfare provision, had pushed up the US government's budget deficit, the size of the public sector and, crucially, inflation.

Richard Nixon succeeded Johnson as US President in 1969, and on 15 August 1971 he decided unilaterally to close the gold window – the facility which gave other central banks the right to buy gold at the fixed price. Nixon's New Economic Policy marked the start of a more bitter stage in international economic relations. Countries now began to be more explicit about pursuing their national interests. The Americans became frustrated at having to deal with the Europeans, who, in Washington's view, could never agree among themselves. The Europeans for their part found the US heavy-handed and unnecessarily aggressive. Britain and Japan, for different reasons, tended to watch many of these conflicts from the sidelines. Attempts were made to patch things up when Nixon forced America's allies to accept a devaluation of the dollar against the other currencies in the Smithsonian Agreement of December 1971. But the newly agreed rates lasted only a short time.

Soon currencies were 'floating': that is, left to have their value determined by the market instead of having a specific value to which a government was committed. In early 1972 the six founder members of the EEC tried to set up their own co-operative arrangement. They set up a joint float: each committed itself to keeping within 2.25 per cent either side of a central rate against each other, so that they would move more or less together against the US dollar. This was known as the snake (because when plotted graphically that is what these currency movements looked like). Again, Britain initially stayed on the sidelines. Sterling then briefly but disastrously joined the snake: only to leave after six weeks at a cost to the foreign exchange reserves of $2.6 billion – a huge figure at the time. This was a period of considerable upheaval for the world's monetary system.

The oil shock

But these problems were temporarily overshadowed by a shock to the world economy on a scale not seen since the end of the Second World

War. In 1973, war broke out between Israel and its Arab neighbours. This had two major economic consequences for the West. The first was short-lived: Arab oil producers co-operated to impose a ban on oil exports to countries they saw as too supportive of Israel – the US, Japan and the Netherlands being worst affected. This lasted for three months and caused much temporary disruption. But much more disruptive and much longer lasting was the sharp rise in oil prices which the Organisation of Petroleum Exporting Countries (OPEC) now chose to impose.

Higher oil prices had been expected for some time, as demand for oil had grown during the boom years and the oil producers had strengthened their cartel; the war simply precipitated the price rises, which had a devastating impact on the world economy because of their size and the speed with which they were imposed. By January 1974, the price of Arabian light crude (used as an indicator of oil prices more generally) was 350 per cent higher than a year earlier, with most of the increase coming in the last two months of 1973. The severity of the impact reflected the greatly increased dependency of Western countries on imported oil: by 1973 it accounted for half their energy needs, double the level in 1950.

The oil exporters, mostly developing countries, saw a correspondingly huge rise in their export revenues. The Arab oil producers, most of which had very small populations, found themselves enormously rich. Producers with much larger populations, such as Venezuela, Nigeria and Indonesia, also benefited enormously. But most developing countries were not oil producers, and they suffered a double blow. They faced a massive increase in their import bill and a sharp fall in their export revenues: the price of non-oil commodities had collapsed as the oil shock hit world demand.

The impact of higher oil prices in the industrial countries was equally great. Oil was crucial for modern industrial economies – which is precisely why OPEC's action had been so effective. Consumption was high – for industrial purposes, for domestic heating in many countries and, above all, for the car. The rise in oil prices had an immediate and prolonged impact on consumer price inflation. In the UK and the US, where inflation was already becoming a serious problem, the effect was almost catastrophic. (See Chapters 2 and 5 for further discussion of Britain's long-running problems with inflation.)

The impact on demand was just as swift. Western Europe saw unemployment start to climb – the beginning of problems with European labour markets which still persist. A new phenomenon, stagflation, emerged: a combination of high and rising inflation and high and rising unemployment, which hitherto had been thought impossible. Most industrial economies, including the US, were badly affected, but the long-term impact on Europe was undoubtedly worse; the term *Eurosclerosis* was coined, implying that Europe's ability to generate rapid GDP growth with low inflation and low unemployment had been lost. For the rest of the century, Europe's failure to create new jobs was in marked contrast to the US economy, which showed great resilience and a remarkable ability to overcome the impact of external economic shocks.

Britain turns to Europe

The UK was acutely affected by this downturn in Europe's economic fortunes. After standing aside at the start of the movement towards European integration, successive British governments came pretty quickly to take a different view. Two attempts to join the EEC were made, by a Conservative government in 1961 and by its Labour successor in 1967, both vetoed by the French President, Charles de Gaulle. Once de Gaulle had left power in 1969, however, the path to British entry seemed clear, and the Conservative government of Edward Heath (which took office in 1970) started new negotiations immediately after the 1970 election. The UK joined the Community in January 1973. Domestically, entry was still a controversial issue (the Labour Party in opposition, having failed to obtain membership in 1967, was now opposed to the idea). But one of the most persuasive economic arguments in favour of entry at the time of Britain's accession had been the dynamic benefits to be gained from membership. The six founding members had enjoyed rates of GDP and productivity growth envied by the UK, and which were judged by many economists to be the result of closer integration. As a new member, the UK had hoped to enjoy the same benefits just as they began to seem illusory in the wake of the rise in oil prices.

Economic co-operation renewed

Although the tensions following the collapse of Bretton Woods remained unresolved, the industrial economies continued to believe in the need for international economic co-operation, however bad-tempered relations might become from time to time. This was still an era when governments were interventionist: when they believed that they could and should act to determine economic performance, both domestically and globally. Following a French initiative, the leaders of the big industrial economies began to meet at annual summits (six countries in 1975 – the US, Japan, Britain, France, West Germany and Canada; in 1976 Italy joined the group, which became known as the G-7).

By the mid- to late 1970s a new theory had emerged to justify collective action at the international level. This was the *locomotive* theory: the idea that the larger and more powerful economies should help weaker ones by stimulating domestic demand, which would have a knock-on effect. Attempts to put the theory into practice were made at the 1978 Bonn Summit of the G-7, when the West German Chancellor, Helmut Schmidt, was prevailed upon by US President Jimmy Carter to aim for a rise in West German GDP to 1 per cent higher than had been planned. The circumstances of this agreement were complex and its origins lay in what America's allies saw as deliberate devaluation of the dollar (known as a dirty float, when governments try to influence the financial markets indirectly) to gain competitive advantage. In return for a commitment to action on the dollar, the US won a commitment to faster growth from the most powerful economy in Europe.

As it turned out, the Americans did not manage to halt the slide of the dollar (or even try very hard, in the view of the other industrial countries); and it is not clear that in practice the West Germans did anything more than they had already been planning. The locomotive theory was discredited at both the political level, since it came to be seen as an attempt by the American administration to evade its own responsibilities, and the economic level, since it failed to deliver the desired results. But the deal tells us much about governments' perceptions of their economic powers at the time. In contrast, by the late twentieth century, governments no longer felt able to set a target for growth, believing their economic responsibilities to be confined to matters such as targets for inflation and government borrowing.

A new philosophical framework

The close of the 1970s marked an important stage in the transition to this more limited view of the role of governments, the nature of government and the definition of desirable and workable economic

---

Box 1.2   Milton Friedman

Milton Friedman (born 1912) is one of the twentieth century's best-known economists. He was Professor of Economics at the University of Chicago until 1979 and was awarded the Nobel Prize for Economics in 1976. Friedman's work has been wide ranging but in the world outside academia his biggest influence was on the way governments tackled inflation. Friedman opposed government attempts to smooth out fluctuations in the economy by following the Keynesian prescription of raising or lowering public spending or taxes: in his view this just led to greater economic instability.

As the industrial world struggled with rising inflation in the 1970s, Friedman's view that 'inflation is always and everywhere a monetary phenomenon' gained ground. The way to control inflation, he argued, was to control the supply of money in the economy. Politicians were attracted to this view partly because of the failure of the approaches used until then and partly because of the simplicity of Friedman's approach. Some academics, however, had questioned the soundness of the research on which his conclusions were based.

Attempts in the US and Britain to control inflation by targeting the money supply were not notably successful, partly because of the difficulty of deciding which measure of money to use. Governments gradually abandoned specific targeting during the 1980s, preferring instead to use more eclectic policies to reduce inflation and then keep it low. Friedman's view that the money supply plays a critical role in determining inflation has survived in diluted form: interest rates are still seen as the key policy instrument. And Friedman's view that there is no trade-off between inflation and unemployment (as had previously been thought) has now largely been accepted as conventional wisdom.

---

policy. This time Britain, for three decades the poor relation in terms of economic performance, was at the vanguard of change. The election of Margaret Thatcher in 1979, followed by fellow conservatives Ronald Reagan in the US in 1981 and Helmut Kohl in West Germany in 1982, marked a shift both in the style and rhetoric of government and in the substance of policy.

During the 1970s, Milton Friedman's economic theories had become increasingly influential among conservative thinkers and politicians in several countries (see Box 1.2). Governments had begun to realise that the control of inflation was a crucial element in providing the right

Box 1.3 The Phillips curve

In 1958, A. W. H. Phillips (1914–75), then Professor of Economics at the London School of Economics, published the results of a research project studying wages and unemployment in the UK from 1861 to 1957. Phillips found a close, inverse relationship between wage inflation and unemployment: high inflation was linked to low unemployment and vice versa. The results, when plotted graphically, became known as the *Phillips curve* (see below).

Phillips's findings appeared to offer governments a choice: for a given target rate of unemployment they could determine what the cost in terms of inflation would be. In this way they could expand the economy to reduce unemployment until inflation reached the limit they could live with. By the mid-1960s, however, economists had begun to be suspicious of this trade-off. These suspicions were confirmed when, in the 1970s, both inflation and unemployment rose. Governments too then realised that the idea of a trade-off, however attractive politically, was not helpful in tackling either problem.

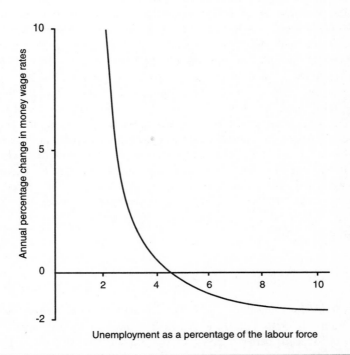

conditions for economic stability and growth. The Phillips curve trade-off, first developed in the 1950s, had appeared to offer governments a choice between inflation and unemployment (see Box 1.3). For obvious political reasons it had been tempting to settle for a bit more inflation in the hope of keeping unemployment low, or bringing it down. The 1970s, however, had demonstrated that the two were not so easily interchangeable. A number of explanations have been offered for this, though, as is so often the case with economic theory, none has been demonstrated conclusively to be right. One view suggests that the immediate post-war decades had seen abnormally low levels of unemployment – 1–2 per cent had come to be regarded in Britain, for instance, as full employment, whereas the Beveridge report in 1942 had judged 3 per cent to be the best attainable figure. But governments had also discovered to their cost that relatively modest rises in inflation were accompanied by much greater instability in the rate of inflation, which could soon start to rise much more rapidly.

Friedman argued that low inflation was a crucial precondition both of stable economic growth and of low unemployment. Moreover, he argued that low inflation was primarily a function of tight control of the money supply. Politicians found his ideas increasingly attractive and convincing. The theory was relatively simple, apparently easy to implement and got governments off the hook of trying to meet high expectations. It was at this point that policy approaches in the industrial countries began to diverge more significantly than possibly at any time since the war. The US and the UK moved towards an increasingly deregulated free market approach to economic policy. Continental European countries, by contrast, tended to favour retention of labour market regulation and provision of more generous welfare systems through higher taxes. Even the European countries, however, strengthened their commitment to tight control of inflation. Indeed, the struggle with inflation became more pressing in the wake of another sharp rise in oil prices, which rose by a further 150 per cent in November 1980.

But it was not so simple

Governments found the world in which they had to manage policy was changing as well – partly as a result of measures they themselves had introduced, partly because of the impact of new technology on economic and social activity. Financial services such as banking, savings, investment and foreign exchange became increasingly sophisticated and rapid. In the US and in the UK this coincided with deliberate moves to deregulate markets. Within six months of the Thatcher government taking office, for example, foreign exchange controls had been abolished completely – people no longer faced restrictions on taking money abroad for holidays or business. Changes were introduced to the structure of the domestic financial system which gave building societies – traditionally the home for long-term domestic savings – more freedom to operate like banks. The extraordinary worldwide growth in the use of credit cards had begun in earnest by this time.

These factors taken together ensured some serious setbacks for the proponents of monetary control within the government. Thatcher and her key advisers, heavily influenced by the ideas of Friedman, had come to power determined to reduce and then control inflation using control of the money supply. They soon found this was nothing like so easy as it sounded. The first problem was defining what you meant by the money supply. Was it the actual cash – notes and coins – moving around the economy? Or did it include some proportion of the money people kept in the bank or building society? Definition was not the only problem. People's behaviour with money was changing rapidly and unpredictably. Within a relatively short time pure monetarism had been discredited.

Inflation in the UK did fall for the first part of the 1980s, but not because the government had successfully implemented the policies it proclaimed. The fall in commodity prices in the wake of the second oil price hike clearly played a part. So too did the high value of the pound at the beginning of the 1980s (a phenomenon initially encouraged by Thatcher on political rather than economic grounds).

Britain and the European Monetary System

But the decline in British inflation was never as impressive as it was in the US or, more significantly at that time, for Britain's European neighbours. In 1979, the European Monetary System (EMS) had been established (see Box 2.5 on page 48): a further attempt to bring some degree of stability to currency movements within Europe, following the collapse of the European snake in 1973. Thatcher's predecessor, James Callaghan, had decided against British membership of the

Exchange Rate Mechanism (ERM), the key part of the EMS intended
to lock exchange rates together; this was a decision which Thatcher
endorsed. Since there was considerable upheaval within the EMS in its
early years, the arguments in favour of Britain joining did not seem
very strong. But the ERM did deliver low inflation for most member
countries. By, in effect, locking currencies and economies more closely
to the German mark, the EMS acted as a powerful anti-inflationary
tool: the mark had an enviable reputation as what is known as a hard
currency – one with very low inflation. The turning point, in a sense,
came with the French decision in 1982 – when many of President
François Mitterrand's socialist objectives were abandoned – to aim for
a *franc fort*, a strong French franc, the equal of the German mark in its
anti-inflationary rigour.

The key European countries, therefore, had low inflation as a
central policy objective and they were, by and large, very successful.
This counter-inflationary success soon brought converts in Britain. By
1984, Nigel Lawson, the British Chancellor of the Exchequer and
previously the architect of the British monetarist experiment, had come
to the view that inflation was best controlled via the exchange rate.
From then on, he argued increasingly forcefully for British membership, engaging in a bitter struggle with the Prime Minister which
culminated in his resignation from the government in 1989. A year
later, Thatcher was finally persuaded, still against her better judgement, to join the ERM (on 8 October 1990), less than two months
before she herself was forced from office (on 27 November 1990). The
UK's membership was short-lived: within two years the pound had
been indefinitely suspended from the ERM. Inflation had declined
during that period, but many economists attributed it to the very high
interest rates which had once again squeezed demand and inflation out
of the economy. The remaining members of the ERM pressed on with
their plans for full Economic and Monetary Union (EMU), which
came to fruition in January 1999. Britain had once again excluded
itself from the move towards greater European integration.

The search for a new consensus

Britain's struggle with both inflation and unemployment for most of
the 1980s underlined the extent to which consensus among policy-
makers at the international level had disappeared. Enormous effort, for

instance, was expended by both policy-makers and academics on trying to understand why Europe was losing jobs at the same time as the US was creating them. Britain was unable to match America's success in job creation even though labour markets in the UK – in contrast to those in continental Europe – were extensively deregulated in the 1980s. US inflation performance was also impressive compared with that of many other industrial countries. But it was not as good as that in Japan, which also managed to record much lower unemployment than any other industrial nation while retaining relatively inflexible labour markets (though at least some of this was attributed by economists to 'hidden' unemployment – disguised by the continuing Japanese tradition of a job for life).

These variations in economic philosophy, policy and performance seemed suddenly and dramatically to diminish in significance in 1989, when the communist system of the Soviet empire collapsed almost overnight. After more than a decade it is hard to imagine – and yet equally hard to overestimate – the symbolic importance of the fall of the Berlin Wall, which signalled the collapse of communism as a potent political force. The economic disparities within the industrialised world seemed minor compared with those of countries which were now liberated neighbours. The shock waves, especially when East Germany was reunited with its far richer Western neighbour in 1990, were felt throughout the world. Effort, attention and resources were diverted to help the former communist economies of Central and Eastern Europe. The ERM came close to the brink of collapse as German monetary policy responded to domestic German needs suddenly different from those of other Western European countries. The UK and Italy were forced out of the ERM in the debacle of September 1992, which created chaos in world financial markets (see Chapters 4, 5 and 8 for a full discussion of these issues).

It soon became clear then that the triumph of capitalism was not quite so overwhelming as the world first imagined. The difficulties of integrating the former communist ('transition') economies into the global economic system have proved considerable. They want help in order to adjust to a free market system; the Western industrial countries urged a rapid move to free markets but were reluctant to open up their own markets to the newcomers. This reluctance has been particularly marked in the European Union (EU) in the protracted negotiations over its proposed significant enlargement to the east. Several of the former communist economies want to be part of this enlargement process, but the access to EU markets which these transition economies so desperately want has, thus far, been slow to materialise.

The problems of most transition economies paled by comparison with Russia's slow and uneven progress towards market liberalisation. Opinions veered widely between optimism that the authorities were determined to transform Russia into a modern market economy and pessimism that they would never be able to deliver this. Reforms became unpopular as GDP contracted, living standards fell sharply and even life expectancy dropped. The prevalence of organised crime discouraged foreign investors. Large amounts of IMF assistance failed to prevent a series of economic upheavals, which caused great anxiety among Western investors in Russia; a large and sudden devaluation of the rouble in 1998 added to the nervousness of Western stock and financial markets. Of all the transition economies, Russia was unique because of its geopolitical role as a nuclear superpower. Because of this, and in spite of its weak economic position, Russia was a regular participant for at least part of every G-7 summit after the break-up of the USSR in 1991.

Crisis in the developing world

The economic turbulence of the 1980s and 1990s also proved unsettling for the developing world. Many countries saw their fortunes fluctuate dramatically. At the beginning of the 1980s, the impact of another round of oil price rises was far worse for the poor countries of the southern hemisphere; the consequences for them – a collapse in demand coupled with falling commodity prices – led to the first Third World debt crisis. Western banks, which had incautiously lent huge sums to some countries, suddenly found themselves dealing with debtor countries which could not pay. Some banks previously thought of as virtually risk free simply collapsed under the weight of irresponsible loans gone bad. Efforts to resolve the twin problems of Western bank exposure and the often desperate plight of countries which had been actively encouraged to over-borrow went on throughout the decade.

The banks failed to learn the lesson of prudence. By the early 1990s, one major preoccupation of the industrial countries was the competitive threat from the so-called Asian tiger economies – countries like South Korea, Taiwan, Singapore, Indonesia, Thailand and Malaysia – which were enjoying spectacular rates of growth. These countries had relatively cheap labour costs coupled with sophisticated manufacturing capacity; they could compete effectively on world markets and were well placed to take advantage of the rapid liberalisation of the world trading system. Foreign capital flooded into them as overseas investors – and banks – saw the prospect of attractive returns. But serious problems surfaced in 1997, when the Thais were forced to devalue their currency in response to adverse market pressures. One collapse followed another and by 1998 most of the tigers were coping with very substantial falls in GDP – of more than 10 per cent in some cases. These economic contractions – far greater than any industrial country had experienced since 1945 – brought real hardship to millions of people. They also threatened to overwhelm the international financial system.

The crisis in Japan

But an even greater threat to the world economy in this period came from Japan, whose economy was, by now, in a parlous state. Decades of political lethargy and incompetence had undermined the achievements of the post-war economic miracle. Questionable practices by many corporations and banks had for many years concealed the effects of a stagnating economy; the problems, when they finally emerged, were by then that much worse. The banks were in a mess. Though interest rates and inflation were remarkably low, Japanese consumers continued to save rather than spend, dragging the economy into a dangerous spiral of decline. Unlike the tiger economies, which, though successful, were still relatively small, Japan was the world's second biggest economy. Its success at exporting combined with the difficulty for foreigners of penetrating the Japanese market had created a huge trade surplus and increased international tensions, most notably with the US and to a lesser extent with Europe. By the late 1990s, there were signs that Japan had begun to get to grips with the worst of its difficulties. But it still faces a prolonged period of adjustment and slow recovery.

Of course, from the perspective of the UK and the other industrial countries, the export success of the Asian tigers and before them Japan had been an important factor in reinvigorating economic behaviour. The need to compete with the Japanese forced companies to overhaul their business practices. The huge investment flows from Japan into many industrial countries, but especially the US and the UK, brought Japanese practices to Europe and North America – ideas such as *just in time* component delivery and *total quality management* revolutionised the workplace in these countries. In the mid-1990s, the UK, for example, became a net car exporter for the first time in nearly thirty years because of the decision of Nissan, Honda and Toyota to set up operations there.

The new world of competition

The end of the post-war policy consensus may have opened up divisions about the best way to manage large industrial economies. But it was accompanied by a growing consensus about how such economies needed to behave in the global economy: competition became the mantra without which no politician could manage. Even when not seen as a Good Thing, competition was seen as inevitable: businesses had to compete nationally and internationally; countries had to compete with each other for jobs, inward investment, economic success. The technology-driven globalisation of industrial activity and the drive to liberalise trade and capital markets contributed to the sense of trying to survive in an economic jungle. In some ways it was all seen as a zero-sum game – only so much of anything was available and if one country did not get jobs from an investment project, another would. Britain worked hard to succeed in attracting overseas investment – during the 1990s it became the second largest recipient of foreign direct investment, after the US. It was also the second largest foreign investor – harking back to the days when late-Victorian Britain had been banker to the world.

In spite of the continuing political emphasis on the importance of trade, investment flows came to dominate international economic activity. Companies were increasingly able to choose the location for activity that suited them, regardless of national boundaries. Manufacturers shifted an increasing amount of their production to Third World countries, whose labour costs were far lower than those of the industrial countries. Industrial economies came to place increasing emphasis on the aspects of economic life to which they could add value: services, especially financial services, intellectual property – ideas – and research and development were expected to account for an

increasing proportion of GDP in these countries, as basic manufacturing shifted elsewhere. Such intense competition had a direct
impact on the macroeconomic policy environment, with increasing
rivalry among national governments as they sought to ensure success
by creating the best environment for corporate investors.

In the late 1990s, the development of the Internet and e-commerce
brought a new impetus to this struggle. E-commerce has made it even
more difficult for government to influence the location of economic
activity. In one sense it can be anywhere and everywhere; and it can be
moved much more quickly than, say, manufacturing production. Significantly, too, Internet activity is not confined to the richer industrial
countries. Much software expertise, for instance, is located in southern
India – an economy which produces many highly qualified workers but
has not, in the past, generated sufficient jobs for them. Now the
location of such expertise is irrelevant for those who need to tap it –
communications technology is eliminating such physical obstacles.

The speed of these changes makes it difficult to predict what shape
the world economy will take in the twenty-first century, and what role
individual national economies will play. Some observers see national
governments and policy-makers as increasingly powerless in the face
of the globalisation of economic activity. Others dispute the extent to
which national sovereignty has been eroded and argue that governments
have considerable scope to affect the future economic development of
their countries by the policies they pursue. In particular, it is increasingly clear that those economies with a highly educated and
skilled workforce are likely to perform much more successfully than
those which lag behind. This is a challenge for policy-makers, and
especially so in Britain, which has a poor record in equipping the
majority of workers with the skills they need. The rest of this book will
examine the challenges facing Britain and how policy-makers have
sought – and are seeking – to meet them.

2   The historical context

We saw, in Chapter 1, the international context in which British policy-makers have had to operate since the Second World War. The last half-century has been a period of intense and rapid change in the global economy, changes which have been reflected both in British society and in public policy. They have also affected the way policy is made in Britain – the principal concern of this book. What follows provides an overview of the way policy and policy-making have changed in Britain since the war. Subsequent chapters will examine policy from an analytical perspective, but the first stage in under-standing how policy is made in contemporary Britain is to understand what went before.

Britain's economic decline

Recent research has questioned the extent of Britain's economic decline before the Second World War. There is little argument, though, that by 1945 the UK economy faced enormous problems. Although Britain had won the war, it had done so at high cost. There was considerable physical damage: houses, factories, roads and ports in many parts of the country were in urgent need of repair because resources had been diverted to the war effort. The success Britain had had in switching the economy on to a war footing left formidable challenges in switching it back to peacetime activity again. The country was in debt to the US: although most of the funds provided to it under the lend–lease arrange-ments were never repaid, in 1945 the UK had been forced to borrow further huge sums – $3.75 billion from the US and $1.25 billion from Canada – in order to meet its financial obligations. Overseas invest-ments, once the provider of substantial and significant capital inflows and which therefore enabled the UK to buy goods from overseas, had been run down to finance the war and were a fraction of their pre-war value. Before the war, in the protectionist world of the 1930s, the Imperial Preference system had offered special terms to countries trading with each other within the British Empire. This system had been dismantled as part of the post-war settlement. Britain was now committed, along with the rest of the world, to opening up markets to trade and competing on equal terms with other countries in the global economy.

Rising domestic expectations

At the same time, the incoming Labour government, headed by Clement Attlee, had to respond to social expectations that had been transformed by the war. The strength of the British effort in the war was, to a considerable extent, the result of an implicit bargain between the political elite and the working classes, who had been particularly badly affected by the depression and high unemployment of the 1930s. It was accepted by both sides of the political divide that there would have to be fundamental changes in the way society was organised after the war. We have already noted the extent of the changes to the international order which were set in train long before the end of the war. Ambitious long-term planning was also under way on the domestic policy front. The Beveridge committee on social security and its report, *Social Insurance and Allied Services* (published in November 1942), set the scene for radical changes to the provision of welfare – pensions and unemployment benefit – which had a lasting impact on UK policy. This report, too, led to the commitment to full employment, contained in the May 1944 White Paper entitled *Employment Policy*, which governments of all parties accepted for more than thirty years:

> The government accept as one of their primary aims and responsi-
> bilities the maintenance of a high and stable level of employment after
> the war.... Total expenditure on goods and services must be prevented
> from falling to a level where general unemployment appears.

Such changes would not have been possible without an accompanying intellectual shift among the policy-making elite. There was widespread acceptance that pre-war economic policy had failed to deal with problems such as high unemployment and poverty. The focus on low inflation which had governed the monetary policy of the Bank of England in the 1930s, coupled with the prevailing belief that it was not the job of governments actively to intervene in the economy, was blamed for the hardship suffered by many during the depression years. By the 1940s, the arguments advanced by Keynes in his *General Theory* (see Box 1.1, page 7) had become more widely accepted. Keynes himself might not have recognised many of the macroeconomic policies pursued in his name in the post-war years. But he had argued that governments had a role to play in stimulating demand at the approb priate time in the economic cycle, and this is what people tended to remember.

Labour's ambitious plans – and disappointments

The desire for a fundamental shift in social and economic policy in 1945 was clearly a key factor in the landslide Labour victory in the general election of that year, in spite of the personal popularity of the Conservative leader, Winston Churchill. Many of the policies in Labour's campaign were developed during Churchill's wartime coalition government, which comprised both Conservative and Labour ministers. But Labour seemed better placed to carry out many of the promised reforms, to which was added the creation of a national health service, outlined in Labour's manifesto. The heady atmosphere of those first post-war days added to the momentum and raised expectations still further. Labour pressed on rapidly – too rapidly in the view of many later analysts – with plans for pension, welfare and health care reform. It pushed forward plans for nationalisation of large sections of the economy – *the commanding heights* – such as public utilities, rail, the coalmines and iron and steel.

It took ministers some time to realise the full extent of Britain's economic weakness, which would make accomplishment of their domestic objectives so much more difficult than they anticipated. They were keenly aware not just of their desire to implement the structural reforms they had promised, but of the need for them to fulfil the expectations they had helped to create. It gradually became obvious that they would not be able to meet these popular demands as quickly as planned, if at all. The new government faced the constraints of a weak external position, made worse by the additional burden of the loans from the US and Canada. Because of this, they were obliged to continue with the system of wartime rationing (which lasted until 1953–4); indeed, rationing was introduced for some items, such as bread, only after the war had ended. Fuel shortages in the freakishly cold winter of 1947 brought home to the electorate and policy-makers alike quite how difficult the economic situation was.

The very substantial devaluation forced on Britain in 1949 (see Box 2.1) made things even more difficult. Crucially, this event sapped the morale of the government's senior ministers still further. Their attempts to control policy, to maintain the initiative, seemed more futile than

---

Box 2.1 Labour and devaluation

On 18 September 1949, the pound was devalued by 30 per cent, from £1 = $4.03 to £1 = $2.80. The decision was forced on a reluctant government: the old rate could no longer be defended, since Britain had insufficient gold and foreign exchange reserves and was facing an acute balance-of-payments deficit. Prime Minister Clement Attlee and his Chancellor, Sir Stafford Cripps, had postponed the decision as long as they could since they saw devaluation as politically damaging. But the delay meant Britain's room for manoeuvre was limited by the time the decision had to be made.

When Labour returned to power in 1964 the new government was determined at all costs to avoid devaluation. The Wilson government – Wilson above all – did not want another Labour government to be saddled with the reputation for devaluing: Wilson did not want Labour labelled for ever as the party of devaluation.

Yet this was the wrong lesson to have taken from the 1949 episode. Just as in 1949 the economic arguments had been strongly in favour of a downward adjustment in the pound's value, so they were in 1964. The balance-of-payments situation – Labour inherited record deficits from the outgoing Conservative government – underlined the damage being done to Britain's competitive position. It is now clear that Treasury officials, the Chancellor's personal economic advisers and some Labour ministers considered the devaluation option on several occasions between 1964 and 1967; but right until the moment when it became inescapable, the Prime Minister himself was opposed.

The result was the impression of a government forced to act against its wishes at a time of crisis – just like the 1949 episode – and so helped to undermine its political authority.

before. These factors, difficult to quantify, were nevertheless important. This was a Cabinet full of men who were already exhausted by the war, in many cases in poor health, and who were finding it increasingly difficult to push through their radical agenda. The extent of the compromises they were forced to make was highlighted by the decision to introduce some charges within the National Health Service (NHS) in 1951. This helped precipitate the resignation from the Cabinet of several key figures, including the future Prime Minister, Harold Wilson. The decision had been taken because of budgetary pressures made worse by rearmament spending as a result of Britain's involvement in the Korean conflict: but the charges were seen as an abandonment of the government's commitment to free health care at the point of delivery.

Labour's legacy

Yet it would be mistaken to overemphasise the gloom of the immediate post-war years. It is true that Labour policy-makers found themselves unable to deliver some of their most important commitments. It is also true, however, that the commitment to full employment was accomplished. Shortly after the end of the war, at a time when labour market difficulties might have been anticipated with the rapid demobilisation of so many military conscripts, unemployment was remarkably low: compared with an inter-war average of more than 10 per cent, unemployment averaged just 1.8 per cent between 1945 and 1970. Inflation was relatively subdued, in spite of the increased emphasis on government intervention in the economy. The NHS was established. Pensioners found themselves better off in real terms than ever before.

With hindsight it can be argued that many of these policies were storing up trouble for the future; by failing to tackle fundamental problems such as Britain's poor productivity performance, the post-war government was simply postponing difficult decisions. Yet the Attlee government established a policy framework which went largely unchallenged for decades. It prepared the ground for a bipartisan approach to key elements of economic policy which ensured that governments became increasingly involved in all sectors of the economy – and were content to encourage expectations which they could often not fulfil. For years, party political arguments about economic policy were largely, though not wholly, about competence rather than underlying policy. Many of the policy instruments which were sub-sequently discredited, and which came to be despised by the political right, were introduced by Conservative governments which followed Labour's lead.

The Conservative approach

Churchill's Conservative government, which inherited the Labour leg-acy, came to power in 1951, at a time when the economic outlook was distinctly brighter. Rationing was coming to an end. Unemployment and inflation remained low. The Tories were opposed to nationalisation in principle, but in practice took no steps to unwind state ownership of the utilities or British Rail, denationalising only the steel industry (the necessary legislation was introduced in 1951 and came into effect in 1953). High taxation was also anathema to the Conservatives but again, in practice, the governments of Churchill, Eden, Macmillan and Douglas-Home, stretching over thirteen years, did little more than tinker with the tax policies they inherited from Labour. Income tax rates were seen as a useful way of regulating demand, as were taxes on the purchase of goods. Public spending rose under the Tories just as it had under Labour. Consumption began to be seen as a politically desirable end in its own right. It was the golden age – in 1957, the Prime Minister, Harold Macmillan, claimed in a subsequently much misquoted phrase, 'most of our people have never had it so good'.

This was, then, the era of what became known as *Butskellism*, a term combining the names of the Conservative Chancellor of the Exchequer under Churchill, R. A. Butler, and the Shadow Chancellor, Hugh Gaitskell, and implying that, in economic policy terms, the two major political parties were indistinguishable. As we saw in Chapter 1, the industrial world had come round to the idea that governments both could and should influence the economy in very direct ways for the benefit of their citizens. There was a widespread belief in the value of public spending on education, health and welfare. There was also a growing conviction, borne out of the experience of the 1930s and the apparent success of post-war policies, that managing demand in the economy was both feasible and desirable. When the economic cycle turned down, and growth slowed, the government's job – or, more specifically, the Chancellor's job – was to touch the accelerator – raise spending, cut taxes – in order to stimulate the economy and stave off the threat of recession and high unemployment. But an ever-vigilant Chancellor also had to watch for those times when growth accelerated too .much, when unemployment fell and inflation threatened to pick up: then it was his job to put his foot on the brake, to raise taxes and cut spending. Treating the economy as if it were a car is perhaps appropriate given the words of one Chancellor who likened his job to that of a driver in the middle of a storm trying to cope without windscreen wipers.

Fine-tuning the economy

The old preoccupation with balancing the books had gone. No longer were taxes raised to ensure sufficient revenues to offset public spending. No more did public spending plans take account of projected tax revenues. Of course, they did to some extent, and to deny this is to exaggerate the extent of the change. But how tax and spending decisions were taken had fundamentally changed. These were factors now seen largely in isolation from each other. They were, above all,

---

Box 2.2   The regulator

The regulator was introduced in 1961 by the Chancellor, Selwyn Lloyd. It gave Chancellors the power to make some adjustments to fiscal policy without having to wait for parliamentary approval. In theory, there were two regulators:

1   the first enabled the Chancellor to raise or lower indirect taxes by up to 10 per cent, with retrospective parliamentary approval needed within three weeks;
2   the second allowed the Chancellor to add an extra amount, of up to 4 shillings (20 pence) a week, to employers' National Insurance contributions.

The second regulator was heavily criticised at the time and was never used in practice. But the indirect tax regulator was used several times in the 1960s. It was designed to give Chancellors the ability to respond quickly to perceived changes in the economy, though with hindsight it is clear that such changes could hardly be conducive to economic stability or helpful to industry.

Table 2.1 Rising living standards in the UK, 1945–70 (in millions)

	Private cars	*Telephones*	*Television licences*
1945	1.5	3.9	–
1950	2.3	5.4	0.3
1955	3.5	6.8	4.5
1960	5.6	8.2	10.5
1965	8.9	10.6	13.2
1970	11.5	14.9	15.9

Data from B. M. Mitchell, *International historical statistics: Europe 1750–1993* (4th edn, Macmillan, 1998).

instruments of economic policy, not of budgetary rectitude. Thus, such ingenious devices such as the *regulator* (introduced in 1961) were developed. This was an automatic stabiliser which varied certain tax rates without the need for parliamentary approval and it was frequently used as part of the effort to *fine-tune* the economy (see Box 2.2).

This approach to macroeconomic management also came to be known as stop–go economics: the belief that a government could judge so precisely when the economy needed a small boost and when it needed to slow down. For a long time many citizens, or consumers as they came to be known, felt very much better off, partly because post-war economic policies tended to distribute income and wealth more evenly – or less unevenly. Material standards rose inexorably (see Table 2.1). Britain in the late 1950s and 1960s in many ways felt like an affluent society – especially for those who remembered the deprivations of the 1930s and the war.

The cost of failure

But there were fundamental weaknesses in the approach of policy-makers. Many of the policies being pursued were to have significant economic costs in the future. There was a trade-off between present gain and future pain. This was partly because neither the post-war Labour administration nor its successors were able or willing to tackle long-term structural problems such as poor productivity growth, which harmed the prospects for Britain's economic growth and trade performance. Britain had been the first economy to industrialise. As a

Box 2.3   The UK's relative economic decline

The figures compare the UK's economic performance with that of the other main industrial countries: between 1950 and 1992, only US productivity growth was slower than that of the UK.

Productivity: GDP per hours worked
(annual average compound percentage growth rate)

	1913–50	*1950–73*	*1973–92*
France	1.9	5.1	2.7
Germany	0.6	6.0	2.7
US	2.5	2.7	1.1
Japan	1.9	7.7	3.1
UK	1.6	3.1	2.2

GDP growth (annual average compound percentage growth rate)

	1950–73	*1973–94*
France	5.0	2.1
Germany	6.0	2.2
US	3.9	2.5
UK	3.0	1.7

Number of years in which GDP fell below previous peak

	1950–73	*1973–94*
France	0	2
Germany	1	3
US	2	4
UK	1	8

From Angus Maddison, *Monitoring the world economy 1820–1992* (OECD, 1995).

relatively small economy, it was bound to be overtaken as other and bigger countries followed the same path. Relative decline, in terms of Britain's share of total world output and world trade, was inevitable – it was evident from around 1870 onwards. The British share of world manufacturing exports, for example, fell from 32.5 per cent in 1899 to 20.4 per cent in 1954 and to around 8 per cent in the 1980s; the share of world merchandise exports went from 10.5 per cent in 1950 to 5.1 per cent in 1997.

The difficulty was deciding how much of this relative decline was unavoidable and how much resulted from weaknesses in the British economy itself. By international standards the UK's growth rate had long been relatively low. For a time, that did not matter so much because the economy was starting from a much higher base than that of other countries. But in the post-war period this decline accelerated. Specifically, UK productivity – the amount produced by each worker per unit of time – grew at an alarmingly slow pace, given the technological changes taking place in the world (see Box 2.3). But the supply side of the economy (essentially, that part of the economy concerned with the production of goods and services as opposed to the demand for them) was largely neglected by policy-makers preoccupied with what they saw as their new-found ability to manage the economy by managing demand. With hindsight, they were simply buying time, postponing the point at which issues such as poor productivity performance would have to be tackled.

Industrial relations

Coincident with this failure – and in hindsight clearly related to it – was the failure to tackle the growing problem of poor industrial relations in Britain. Labour's post-war election victory had greatly strengthened the power of the unions; so had the tight conditions in the labour market which had prevailed during the 1950s and 1960s. A longstanding tradition of confrontational management in many sectors of industry encouraged union militancy when employers found themselves struggling to find suitably qualified labour. Pay pressures mounted. By the 1960s, Britain had acquired a reputation, largely deserved, of an economy plagued by strikes and with wage rises running well ahead of both inflation and productivity improvements. Macroeconomic policy was not the only area of economic management run on stop–go lines.

A new approach?

When, after thirteen years in opposition, Labour won power again in
the election of 1964, with Harold Wilson as Prime Minister, there were
echoes of 1945. Wilson came to power amid considerable popular
expectations. He had talked about the need for Britain to become a
modern economy: a year before the general election he had said that
'new Britain would be forged in the white heat of the ... scientific
revolution'.

The size of the balance-of-payments deficit under the last year of
Conservative government – the result, it was argued, of too heavy a
touch on the economic accelerator in the hope of election victory – had
helped tip the balance towards a Labour majority, albeit a very small
one. The new government had radical new plans for dealing with what,
by then, had come to be seen as Britain's principal economic problem:
a failure to grow as fast as other industrial countries.

The cornerstone of the government's new economic policy was
indeed radical: the plan was to remove the Treasury's macroeconomic
policy responsibilities and transfer them to a new department, the
Department of Economic Affairs (DEA). In the search for a scapegoat
for Britain's troubles, some politicians had identified the Treasury as
the problem – too concerned with controlling what the rest of government did, too preoccupied with arcane intellectual inquiry. What was
needed, the advocates of the new arrangements claimed, was to leave
the Treasury with clear responsibilities for spending, taxation and
monetary policy; and to make the DEA responsible for managing the
economy, ensuring that Britain's long-term growth potential was increased.

The DEA's principal tool was to be the new National Plan. This was
finally unveiled in 1965. The idea was to avoid bottlenecks in the
economy caused by industry's inability to cope with upswings in
demand and a shortage of appropriately skilled workers. Activity in the
economy would be planned in great detail, far more than had ever been
attempted before. More than thirty years on, it seems hard to believe
that the project was ever taken seriously. It was; but it was a complete
failure and the great idea was soon allowed to die as quietly as possible
to save the government's face. This was easier than expected because
of the rapid political decline of the plan's principal sponsor, George
Brown (Secretary of State for Economic Affairs), and because the
crisis of devaluation soon overtook the government.

Devaluation crisis

In 1966, the Wilson government was re-elected with a handsome majority. But by the following year it was clear that, far from tackling the fundamental economic problems facing Britain, the government was presiding over a serious deterioration. Industrial relations had worsened as public sector workers assumed that a Labour government, so dependent on the political support of the unions, would support them. Often it was: pay rises in both the public and private sector continued to rise well above the rate of inflation. Britain's external

---

Box 2.4 *In Place of Strife*

During the 1960s, industrial relations deteriorated sharply, with the growing number of unofficial strikes – those not properly authorised by the relevant trade union – being a particular problem. In 1965 the Wilson government established the Royal Commission on Trade Unions and Employers Associations to examine what could be done. Its report (known as the Donovan report, after the Commission's chairman) was published in June 1968. It accepted the need for reform but rejected the use of law and instead favoured the registration of collective bargaining agreements with the Department of Employment.

But the new Secretary of State for Employment and Productivity, Barbara Castle (appointed in April 1968), felt the Donovan report did not go far enough. She produced a White Paper in January 1969, *In Place of Strife*, with much tougher proposals. Castle wanted to make unions responsible – and liable to fines – in the event of unofficial strikes. The government, not the employers, would initiate action in such cases. The Employment Secretary would also have the power to require a strike ballot; to order a 28-day conciliation period; and to impose a settlement in certain cases.

Castle was strongly supported by Harold Wilson, the Prime Minister. But her plans split the Cabinet, with James Callaghan (by then Home Secretary) one of the most vociferous opponents. After a series of bitter rows Wilson finally negotiated a compromise with the Trades Union Congress, which gave a 'solemn and binding' undertaking to intervene in unofficial disputes. The Trades Union Congress claimed that it kept its word and that it did succeed in reducing the number of such strikes. But the outcome was widely seen as a defeat for Wilson and Castle, who had been forced to abandon their plans for statutory measures.

---

financial position was, by now, acute. The government had several times used the lending facilities of the IMF to ease its balance-of-payments difficulties. But international concern about the government's problems manifested itself as downward pressure on the pound, no matter how hard the government tried to resist it. Devaluation continued to be seen as political weakness, however. For Prime Minister Wilson, it was a taboo subject: even discussion of it was forbidden.

In spite of every effort to avoid devaluation, the government was finally obliged to concede defeat in November 1967. The Chancellor, James Callaghan, resigned soon afterwards. The sense of political humiliation which accompanied the crisis left a lasting impression on all politicians. This view of devaluation as political failure heavily influenced policy-makers in 1992, when the Conservative government was trying hard to keep sterling within the ERM.

Although devaluation had a beneficial impact, the policies which accompanied it proved less effective than they could have been. The UK's balance-of-payments position certainly improved as exports became cheaper and thus more competitive abroad, while imports were more expensive in relation to domestically produced goods. The new Chancellor, Roy Jenkins, determined to recover a grip on the economy, introduced a series of tight budgets designed to curb public spending, raise taxes and reduce the government's budget deficit, as well as strengthen the external position. By the time of the 1970 election, the outlook for the economy seemed more favourable than it had been for some time. But Jenkins had not taken sufficiently firm action to combat inflation, which was now becoming a more serious problem. And the Wilson government had failed to tackle the rapidly worsening state of Britain's industrial relations (see Box 2.4).

The troubles mount

In spite of the conventional wisdom of the post-war years, that governments lose elections only when the economy is performing badly (and which had helped exaggerate the stop–go approach to economic management), Labour lost the election and Edward Heath's Conservative government took power. This coincided with accelerating economic decline. Industrial relations worsened dramatically because of the new government's determination to introduce legislation to curb strikes, using a new Industrial Relations court to impose statutory limits on union power (including swingeing fines). This legislation was strongly, sometimes violently opposed and ensured that militant public sector unions, particularly the electricity workers and the miners, were able to deal fatal blows to the government as other economic developments brought the economy to the brink of collapse.

Heath and his government had ambitious plans for creating a much more entrepreneurial society, to revive Britain's economic fortunes. The Conservatives became committed to what they called 'disengagement' from government intervention in the economy. The idea was to curb public spending and reduce the penal rates of tax on those who were meant to be at the vanguard of this economic change. It would mean an end to the government (or the taxpayer) bailing out firms which were in trouble and to Labour's approach of trying to 'pick winners': firms for which state aid could be justified because their success would benefit the national economy.

But the Heath government's aims were thwarted – like many of those of its predecessors – by developments it found it could not control. Inflation in particular was becoming a serious cause for concern; after the 1967 devaluation it had gradually crept up until it reached 6.5 per cent in 1970 – the highest rate since the early 1950s. In 1971 it rose sharply, to 9.5 per cent. The need for action to curb inflationary pressures became more pressing. But a more serious problem – at least in political terms – manifested itself. For the first time since the war, unemployment started to rise sharply: up from 3 per cent in 1970 to 3.8 per cent in 1971 and 4.2 per cent the year after. The number out of work passed the one million mark in January 1972. These rises were unprecedented and, as the Chancellor at the time, Anthony Barber, said, 'paradoxical'. Inflation and unemployment were not supposed to rise sharply at the same time.

The Heath U-turn

No post-war government had questioned the commitment to full employment; nor, in spite of its aims of disengagement, did the Heath government. In what came to be seen as a dramatic U-turn, the government abandoned many of its election commitments. By early 1972, it had jettisoned the idea of disengagement and embarked on a policy of state intervention in industry. It injected demand into the economy to reverse the rise in unemployment. As a result of cuts in the tax burden and increases in public spending, the economy began to grow more rapidly than it had for many years – and more rapidly than many economists reckoned was possible without fuelling inflation. They were right. Although inflation fell back slightly in 1972, this was only a temporary respite. Capitulation to high wage demands from public sector workers, including miners and power workers, who were willing to strike and cause widespread disruption in pursuit of their claims, added impetus to the inflationary spiral.

By 1973, the government's about-turn was complete; but it had lost control of events. There was now a statutory prices and incomes policy – legally enforceable limits on both price increases and pay rises. As a result of the government's measures, the economy was growing at an unprecedented rate (GDP grew by 7.1 per cent in 1973). But inflation was soaring and unemployment, though it had fallen back a little, was still high. Then came the most serious blow to the government's efforts to regain its grip: the oil price shock of 1973. As we saw in Chapter 1, this had a devastating impact on the global economy. But with Britain already experiencing rates of inflation far higher than other industrial countries, the result of the swingeing increases in the price of crude oil fed rapidly through the economy. Recession followed.

An economy in crisis

This inflationary culture long outlived the Heath government. Britain has had one of the most protracted struggles with inflation of any industrial country in the late twentieth century and only in the late 1990s was there some evidence that attitudes – and economic realities – had fundamentally changed (see Chapter 5). But if the Heath government was not the only political victim of the British battle with inflation, it was arguably the first. By the winter of 1973–4 the economy was in severe crisis. It may seem like an exaggerated statement when made from such a distance, but the government's struggle with the unions, in particular the miners, did raise some fears that the foundations of British democracy were being undermined and that political anarchy was a real possibility.

At the heart of the problem was the determination of the miners to defeat the government's incomes policy, at least insofar as it applied to them. In the early 1970s, the miners were a large and potent political force, even though a substantial programme of pit closures during the

1960s had already reduced their numbers from around 700,000 to about 300,000. They demanded a much larger pay rise than the government was prepared to countenance. Ministers' principal anxiety was that the miners would set a precedent which other unions would seek to follow, a fear which they claimed was not alleviated by the declaration of the Trades Union Congress (TUC) that other unions would treat the miners as a special case and not seek to obtain similar pay rises. The government also clearly saw this fight as a test of its political authority and in so doing badly misjudged the mood of the electorate. With the country on a three-day working week (to conserve energy); the prospect of power cuts; the impression of a government unable to get to grips with inflation; and growing worries about political instability, the popular mood was more complex than it first appeared. A snap election in February 1974 led to the government's defeat, and another victory for the – surprised – Labour leader, Harold Wilson.

The Labour inheritance

Labour was largely unprepared for office and it had no radical new ideas on how to tackle inflation. The new government had entered into a 'Social Contract' with the unions as part of its election manifesto. Its

Table 2.2 Inflation in the 1970s (year-on-year change in average annual rate)

Year	Percentage rate
1969	5.4
1970	6.4
1971	9.4
1972	7.6
1973	9.2
1974	16.1
1975	24.2
1976	16.5
1977	15.8
1978	8.3
1979	13.4
1980	18.0

Data from the *Employment Gazette* (Department for Education and Employment, various issues).

better relationship with union leaders enabled it to settle the miners' strike quickly. Labour maintained a version of the Heath prices and incomes policy, and introduced subsidies on food to try to exert some downward pressure on inflation. There was also some artful juggling with the official figures to create the impression that inflation was falling during the summer, which helped Labour to win a more convincing majority in a second election in October 1974. But the underlying problem did not go away: inflation continued to rise sharply, amid much talk of hyperinflation. In August 1975, year-on-year inflation reached 26.9 per cent (see Table 2.2).

The Europe issue settled

The preoccupation with domestic economic and political problems during the mid-1970s tended to overshadow the development of which Heath was most proud and which is certainly his lasting achievement – the entry of the UK into the EEC (as it was then) in 1973. As noted in Chapter 1, this was – and still is – a hugely divisive issue for Britain, although the divisions have never followed clear party lines. Nevertheless, when in opposition in the 1970s, the official Labour Party line had been to oppose entry and the new government came to power committed to undertake a renegotiation of the terms of entry. In 1975, the new terms – with largely cosmetic differences – were the subject of a referendum which resulted in a massive endorsement of the government's recommendation to stay in the EEC. (See Chapter 4 for a fuller discussion of this.)

The 1976 IMF crisis: origins

Although Labour stayed in office for more than five years, Wilson – unexpectedly – resigned in March 1976, to be succeeded by James Callaghan. Within months, his administration faced a major economic and political crisis, one which had a lasting impact on the Labour Party and which helped pave the way for the long period of Conservative government in the 1980s and 1990s. In part, at least, the difficulties stemmed from the rapid rise in public spending seen during the 1970s and particularly after the 1974 election. The resource-based structure of public spending adopted in the 1960s had, on the whole, worked well during the period of low inflation – indeed, it had been the envy of many industrial countries (see Chapter 9, page 173). But at a time of rapidly rising inflation, guaranteeing public spending plans in real terms simply added to the difficulties of curbing inflationary pressures. The government's spending bill soared. The problems this created for economic management had somewhat belatedly been recognised and by the mid-1970s the Treasury was introducing cash limits on departmental spending plans: if inflation rose by more than anticipated, spending departments would not get all the extra cash they needed.

But this mechanism took some time before it began to have an impact and even then the system as initially introduced had weaknesses. It was not until the 1980s that a system of cash control on public spending which had the necessary teeth was finally introduced. Moreover, Labour, swept into office unexpectedly, had had no time to jettison some of its hugely expensive electoral commitments. Public sector pay rises and food subsidies added to the upward pressure on public spending. The Public Sector Borrowing Requirement (the amount a government needs to borrow to bridge the gap between public spending and tax revenues) had soared. At the same time, the economy – battered by the impact of inflation, widespread industrial unrest and a sense of perpetual crisis reinforced by a seemingly endless series of mini-budgets (there had been four main budgets and five mini-budgets by the middle of 1976) – was losing international confidence. The UK's competitive and trading position seemed to be deteriorating at alarming speed: the balance-of-payments surplus left by the Labour Chancellor Roy Jenkins in 1970 had swung rapidly into deficit from the time of the Heath government's U-turn as imports surged while exports failed to keep pace. The external position was weak and getting weaker: the balance-of-payments deficit was by now unsustainable.

The IMF crisis: outcome

In the late autumn of 1976, the government found itself obliged to go to the IMF for balance-of-payments support. This was not, of course, the first time a British government had done so; and it was, after all, what the IMF was for. But for loans of the size Britain needed ($3.9 billion, the largest it had ever sought from the Fund), IMF assistance was what is known as 'conditional': there were strings attached.

In return for the temporary assistance which the government needed, the IMF demanded swingeing cuts in government spending, the aim being to ensure that Britain's fundamental economic problems were tackled properly. This caused a crisis within the government, with some ministers willing to follow the IMF prescription but others furious at the idea that a Labour government could renege on all that it had previously stood for.

In retrospect, of course, this was the last stand (at least in government) for the old school of economic thinkers who believed that high levels of public spending were a central part of economic management. It was a sign that the old consensus approach to economic policy had vanished completely. The realists within the government took the view that there was no alternative but to comply with the IMF's demands: Britain was not and never could be an autarkic economy. It depended heavily on trade, both imports and exports. Immediately before the crisis erupted, Prime Minister Callaghan had issued an unprecedented and bold warning to the Labour Party conference:

> For too long we postponed facing up to fundamental choices and fundamental changes in our society and our economy.... We used to think you could spend your way out of a recession.... I tell you in all candour that that option no longer exists, and that insofar as it ever did exist it only worked ... by injecting a bigger dose of inflation into the economy followed by a higher level of unemployment. That is the history of the last twenty years.

That view prevailed in the ensuing negotiations both within the government and with the IMF.

Not a real crisis?

The IMF crisis is a particularly powerful example of the problems which governments and policy-makers face. They have to deal with and respond to the facts as they appear at the time. The picture may not always be accurate, however: figures produced at the time are subject to revision – often very substantial revision – as the statisticians try to correct and refine them in the light of new information. This is what happened in 1976. Once final revisions to the economic data had been made, it became clear that the economy was in considerably better shape than assumed at the time. Public spending was being more effectively controlled via the new system of cash limits than anyone had realised. The external position was not quite so weak as the statisticians had thought. By then, however, it was too late. Labour was committed to a new economic strategy imposed on it by the IMF: public spending curbs and the introduction of monetary targets in order to bring inflation under control.

Monetarism in Britain

By the mid-1970s, the work of economists like Milton Friedman (see Chapter 1) had begun to influence economic policy in the industrial countries as they tried to eradicate, or at least reduce, inflation. Friedman argued that inflation was primarily a monetary phenomenon – it reflected inadequate control of the money supply. His ideas were already being taken up by Margaret Thatcher, leader of the Conservative Party since 1975, and her advisers. But it is worth remembering that Denis Healey, Chancellor in Callaghan's Labour government, was the first to preside over monetary targeting in Britain (and met his targets more successfully than the subsequent Conservative government).

Another incomes policy failure

By the late 1970s, the British economy was looking in better shape: but although inflation had started to come down (to 8.3 per cent in 1978), it remained a problem. The Callaghan government had stuck with an incomes policy as a way of helping curb inflation but, in spite of Labour's close links with the trade unions, Callaghan became another electoral victim of the industrial relations crisis. The Prime Minister, who had struggled to remain in office with Liberal Party support ('the Lib–Lab pact'), decided against an election in autumn 1978. The government wanted to introduce a 5 per cent limit on pay rises in an attempt to bring inflation under control. Since the trade unions would not agree, it was left to the government to impose the limit on its own (very large) workforce. This prompted a rash of public sector strikes – including refuse collectors and cemetery workers, and 1978–9 became known as the 'winter of discontent'. When the election finally came, in May 1979, the Conservative leader, Margaret Thatcher, became Prime Minister with an agenda for radical reform.

Thatcher's radical new approach

The Conservative Party swept to power with the failures of the Heath government (in which she had been Education Secretary) a vivid memory for the new Prime Minister. She was determined not to be swayed by events in the way that she believed Heath had been: 'the lady's not for turning' became one of her most famous utterances. Thatcher was a passionate believer in free markets. She had also become a monetarist believer: she detested inflation and was determined to curb it once and for all by controlling the money supply. She wanted to cut public spending and borrowing. She was also convinced of the need to tackle the supply side of the economy. The idea was to create the capacity for faster growth in the economy by making much more rapid improvements in labour productivity; by making labour markets more flexible (by making it easier for workers to move in and out of jobs and for employers to hire and fire people); and by freeing up the entrepreneurial spirit in the economy. It was soon clear how radical the government was determined to be: within six weeks the budget slashed the top rate of income tax from 83 per cent to 60 per cent, and cut the basic rate from 33 per cent to 30 per cent, while raising value-added tax (VAT) from 8 per cent to 15 per cent. Interest rates started to rise as part of the process of controlling monetary growth. The following spring, the government introduced the Medium-Term Financial Strategy, which set out targets for monetary growth and inflation, and for government borrowing (see Box 5.2, page 105).

It also became clear that Thatcher had explicitly abandoned any idea of a commitment to full employment. In her view and that of her advisers, the key to bringing down unemployment was to bring down inflation. In fact, to begin with, inflation rose sharply under the Thatcher administration (it peaked at 21.9 per cent in May 1980). This was partly because of public sector pay deals to which the government had committed itself during the general election campaign. The pound rose sharply as well: investors were attracted by the high interest rates imposed as part of the government's efforts to control the money supply and by Thatcher's public affirmation of her belief in a strong currency.

An old-fashioned recession

Interest rates – already high under the outgoing Labour government – were pushed to unprecedented levels as the government struggled to control the money supply, reaching 16 per cent in July 1980. The result of these moves was a severe recession, which began in 1980, arguably the most severe since the war. The government that had won office pledging to end stop–go economics became hugely unpopular. The business failure rate soared, as did unemployment (on the government's own measure up from 4 per cent in 1979 to 8.1 per cent in 1981). The government stood firm, with the 1981 budget actually increasing the tax burden (although, again, subsequent revisions to the figures showed that there was actually a fiscal relaxation in 1981). The turnaround came by the end of 1981, when the economy finally began to expand once more. Inflation had begun to move down quite sharply, but unemployment continued to rise until it reached 11.2 per cent in 1986. Meanwhile, the money supply rose uncontrollably, no matter what the government did. The link between monetary growth and inflation proved to be more elusive than its advocates had anticipated.

It soon became clear that inflation had been squeezed out of the economy in the old-fashioned way – by a massive contraction in demand. The recovery, which gathered pace from 1982, was also somewhat old-fashioned in its origins – most economists now accept that the depreciation in sterling during the 1980s was substantially responsible for the upturn in demand. This does not necessarily prove the monetarists completely wrong. The trouble with the government's attempts to target the supply of money was that they coincided with major changes in the nature of the economy – some of them, perhaps ironically, the result of other government policies. In 1980 the government relaxed rules on special bank deposits (introduced in 1978 to curb bank lending). This caused an explosion in the money supply much greater than anticipated. Freeing up the building societies and allowing them to act more like banks also meant that measures of the money supply changed fundamentally as consumers' behaviour altered. The measures became unstable just when the government was trying to use them as the centrepiece of its economic strategy.

The world was changing too: international financial markets were becoming more fluid, partly in response to new technology making it easier to switch money across national boundaries, partly because of capital market deregulation, a move wholeheartedly endorsed and encouraged by the Thatcher government. Within a few months of taking office, the government had removed all external capital controls, enabling individuals and businesses to move money to and from the UK whenever they wished. These changes underline one of the principal difficulties of conducting economic policy: it cannot be done in a scientific laboratory – it has to be done in the real world, where other factors will be at work, sometimes moving in a contrary direction.

The British economy transformed?

Monetarism had been quietly abandoned by the mid-1980s. Yet the UK economy and UK economic policy appeared to have undergone a transformation. GDP was expanding rapidly, inflation was falling, productivity had shown dramatic improvements and the government's privatisation programme was in full swing as public utilities and other state assets were shifted into the private sector. In 1983 Thatcher had demonstrated that governments could win elections with high and rising unemployment. Even a year-long miners' strike in 1984–5 – politically controversial and divisive though it was – had little economic impact beyond the communities directly affected. It was all a far cry from the Heath years and the famous uncontrollable Barber boom (presided over by Heath's Chancellor, Anthony Barber), which had fuelled so much of the inflationary pressures in the economy in the 1970s.

Or was it? In fact, the miracle years turned out to be remarkably short-lived. By 1988, it had become clear that not only was the economy booming, but that it was a boom becoming unsustainable. The economy expanded by 4.1 per cent in 1987 and by 4.8 per cent in 1988 – double the rates of growth Britain was accustomed to. But in spite of the political rhetoric, the reformed economy seemed no more capable of expanding at such levels without generating inflationary pressures than it had in the past. Inflation was rising sharply. The Chancellor, Nigel Lawson, famously called the rise a temporary blip, but it became clear this was not the case – it rose to 10.9 per cent in 1990. Interest rates, cut worldwide after the 1987 stock market crash, were progressively raised, to 15 per cent in the autumn of 1989 – close to the 16 per cent record in 1980. Sterling rose too, adding to the problems of businesses trying to sell their goods abroad at increasingly uncompetitive prices and fuelling inflation still further through higher import prices.

The European problem again

At least part of the blame for the inflationary surge was closely bound up with another issue – one which came to dominate the final years of the Thatcher government – the ERM. Most of the UK's EEC partners had joined the ERM (the central element of the EMS) when it was set up in 1979 (see Box 2.5). Both the Callaghan and Thatcher governments had chosen to keep Britain out, for a number of carefully argued reasons. Thatcher's opposition to the ERM grew in line with her antipathy to the European Community. But Lawson became convinced by the mid-1980s that the pound should join the ERM. He believed that, in view of the failure of pure monetarism, an external anchor was the UK's best hope of becoming a low-inflation economy. Economies whose currencies were in the ERM had, according to the Lawson analysis, successfully brought down inflation because of the discipline enforced on them by their link with the German mark. He privately decided to shadow the mark informally: in other words, he secretly aimed to keep the pound at the same rate against the mark, intervening in the foreign exchange markets or adjusting interest rates to ensure this. His target rate was three marks to the pound. But the pound's strength meant that he found himself cutting interest rates to dissuade foreign investors from buying pounds in order to maintain his target rate. This, as it turned out, only helped fuel the inflationary boom. Thatcher – who claimed not to know what was going on – was furious when she discovered Lawson's tactics. Relations between the two steadily deteriorated, with their differences over the ERM becoming more serious. On 26 October 1989, the Chancellor resigned. He was replaced by John Major.

Another old-fashioned recession

The new Chancellor inherited an economy on the brink of another severe recession. The obvious charge to be levelled at the government was that Thatcherism was boom–bust economics by another name. Nothing had fundamentally changed: inflation was squeezed out of the economy the same way as before, with a contraction in demand. The government's borrowing requirement, negative (or in surplus) in the two years from 1988 to 1990 as the government proudly started to repay the national debt, moved rapidly back into deficit – on an almost

Box 2.5   The European Monetary System

The EMS was first proposed at the Copenhagen Summit of EEC heads of government in 1978; the details were fleshed out during that year and it came into being in April 1979. Britain did not join the key feature of the system, the ERM, until 1990.

The aim of the ERM was to reduce currency volatility between the European currencies. Some saw it as a precursor to full economic and monetary union, though this did not become an acknowledged or formal objective until the late 1980s.

The basic principles of the ERM were straightforward, although its technical operation was complex and sophisticated. Each member currency had a central rate against each other member currency, and each government was committed to keeping the value of its currency to within 2.25 per cent either side of that central rate. These were known as the currency bands. An exception was made for Italy, which had a 6 per cent band; this exception was extended to the UK, Spain and Portugal when they joined.

Because of the number of currencies involved (ten at the outset), the actual freedom of movement between one currency and another might be less than the bands implied, since the limits applied to all other currencies. Thus, a currency at the top of its band against one other currency might be closer to its central rate against the rest.

The obligation to keep currencies within their bands was meant to be symmetrical, applying to both currencies involved, the weaker and the stronger. There was an early warning system indicating when one currency moved up or down against another by three-quarters of its permitted margins. The remedy in these cases was intervention in the foreign exchange markets to support weaker currencies or ease upward pressure on stronger ones; and in more extreme cases, domestic policy action, such as changes in interest rates.

The ERM also contained provisions for the central rates themselves to be changed if one or more currencies were felt to be fundamentally misaligned, that is, if they persistently found it difficult to stay within their bands. This happened frequently in the first four years of the ERM's existence (eleven realignments during that period), but much less so after that. The UK often chaired realignment meetings since its non-participation in the ERM gave it a useful neutrality.

Calculating the central rates was a complex business in itself. It was done by reference to a newly created notional currency, the ecu. This was a basket of all EMS member currencies (including the pound): the ecu contained specified proportions of each member currency, and it had an equivalent value in each. The composition of the ecu was reviewed every five years.

unprecedented scale. The totems of good housekeeping fell by the wayside as the government struggled to bring the economy back on track.

The ERM crisis

By the time the recession finally ended and the economy began to expand, Thatcher had been forced out (on 28 November 1990) – the victim of her own unpopular policies on Europe, local taxes and economic failure – and John Major, her successor, had won the 1992 election against all the odds. In what turned out to be the last weeks of her premiership, Thatcher had finally been persuaded by Major to agree to join the ERM (the UK formally joined on 8 October). This was a move widely welcomed at the time, but as the economy stubbornly refused to show signs of picking up, the cost of keeping sterling in the ERM became more and more unpopular. High interest rates in Germany following reunification in 1990 meant high interest rates across Europe as currencies struggled to maintain their ERM parities with the mark. British business bitterly complained about the cost of borrowing and the high value of sterling. Economic confidence was low. A summer of confusion both domestically and in the international financial markets was ended abruptly when the pound was forced out of the ERM – with Britain unable to defend the rate any further. (See Chapters 4, 5 and 8 for further discussion of these issues.)

Comparisons with 1967 were soon made. The collapse of the central plank of the government's economic policy was politically devastating – the Major administration never recovered its political authority. But, to a much greater extent than the 1967 devaluation, the economic benefits were soon apparent. The sharp devaluation of sterling, coupled with the big cuts in interest rates which the government was able to make once there was no ERM parity to defend, provided a significant and rapid boost to economic confidence. Moreover, the Major government, forced to find a replacement for its counter-inflationary policy, came up with what turned out to be a successful alternative. Instead of using the money supply or the exchange rate as a proxy for inflation, the government announced that in future it would target inflation directly and use a combination of policies to reach that target – set at that time at 1–4 per cent over the medium term.

A golden age?

In economic terms, the 1990s took on the appearance of a golden age. Inflation, already relatively low because of ERM membership, continued to fall – to its lowest level for more than thirty years. Interest rates, including real interest rates (i.e. interest rates minus the inflation rate), fell. GDP expanded without appearing to fuel inflationary pressures. Productivity continued to improve. Unemployment started to fall much more rapidly after the 1990–2 recession than it had after that of the early 1980s. It fell from the beginning of 1993 and continued to fall, more or less continuously and often more rapidly than economists expected, to the end of the century.

A new Labour government

The 1997 general election brought Labour back to power after eighteen years. In many respects, the UK economy was in better shape than it had been for decades: inflation, unemployment and interest rates were low and falling. There was a return to some sort of consensus about macroeconomic management, albeit a rather different one than that seen after the Second World War. Politicians from different parties continued to stress their differences, but it was clear that all the major parties were in favour of low inflation, relatively deregulated labour markets, low direct taxes and tight control over public spending. None seemed ready to commit itself to full employment as a specific policy objective. Within days of taking office, the new Labour Chancellor, Gordon Brown, switched responsibility for setting interest rates and achieving the inflation targets to the Bank of England from the Treasury, although the Chancellor continues to decide what the inflation target is. This was seen at the time as something of a political coup for the new government, but it did not of itself fundamentally alter the nature of counter-inflationary policy.

Conclusions

This, then, is the historical context of current British economic policy: inevitably framed by experience and understanding of the past and by domestic and international economic – and political – circumstances.

We have seen, in a broad-brush way, *what* happened, and in some ways *why*. Both of these are relevant concerns of this book. But so too – and crucially – is the *how*. How do governments decide on policy? What are the mechanisms? How do changes in economic thinking permeate through the government machine to affect policy? How are the competing pressures – from political ideology, from external and domestic developments, from short-term political manoeuvring – balanced against each other? How is the final policy decision arrived at? In Chapter 3 we will examine the mechanisms of policy-making, to help find the answers to some of these questions, before looking at some of the specific policy issues in more detail in the subsequent chapters.

3   The structure of policy-making

The policy-making environment

Chapters 1 and 2 have shown something of the background against which public policy has been made over the past half century. The UK is one of the industrial world's most open economies, heavily dependent on trade and on the international financial markets. Policy-makers must therefore take account of the circumstances of and developments in the global economy. These factors, as Chapter 1 made clear, are always powerful influences on domestic policy; they can, in some cases, be overwhelming. They are *exogenous* factors, over which policy-makers have little direct control. There is any number of examples of policy-makers' ambitions being thwarted by unexpected developments elsewhere in the world. A collapse in US stock market prices, a rise in German interest rates, a sharp devaluation of the Thai bhat, a Russian government decision to default on its international loans: these are all events which have had major repercussions for the UK economy and UK policy.

But the domestic policies and developments which make up the historical context in which policy-makers must operate are just as important as the exogenous factors. What has gone before – in terms of both policies and events – critically affects what happens now and in the future. A new policy on unemployment, for example, may affect the level of unemployment at some point in the future: it will not have any impact on the number of people out of work tomorrow or next week. It is the same with inflation. It is generally assumed that there is a time lag between policy action and consequent changes in inflation of about eighteen months to two years. The current rate of inflation reflects policy in the past and nothing a government does today will have much impact on the inflation rate for another two years or so. It is what policy-makers did in the past – and how the various economic actors responded to those policies – which determines where the economy is at any given point in time.

These two groups of factors are of themselves powerful constraints on policy-makers and policy. But there are others; so many, in fact, that it becomes difficult to see how anything like coherent policy ever emerges. A Chancellor with a clear vision of what he wants to do in a specific policy area has a large number of obstacles to cross before any new policy can be successfully introduced. Economic policy cannot be made in a vacuum. Account must be taken of what is happening elsewhere in the world; and any new policies, or changes in policy, must take account of the existing policy framework.

But it does not end there. Economic policy does not depend on the whim or vision of one man or woman. The UK is a parliamentary democracy, with an executive branch run by the Cabinet. The Prime Minister is *primus inter pares* – he or she must secure the agreement of colleagues for major policy initiatives. Any other minister must first have the agreement of the Prime Minister – and then get Cabinet agreement. Of course, there are grey areas. There is much talk of a more presidential style of government these days, implying that the Prime Minister is more powerful, in relation to Cabinet colleagues, than used to be the case. Prime ministers can sack colleagues with whom they have substantial disagreements. But even a powerful and charismatic Prime Minister has to jump through the hoops outlined below. There are, after all, limits on what even presidents can do.

The incremental nature of policy

We have already noted that economic policy cannot be made in a vacuum. We can go further and note that in practice large areas of policy change only gradually and incrementally over time. Economic policy affects almost every aspect of daily life: it can influence whether we have a job, a home, whether we can afford to borrow money, how much we have to spend on essential and non-essential items, whether we can take a holiday abroad, how we manage when we are sick and when we are old – nothing is left untouched.

But at the same time, economic policy is rarely able to determine *any* of these things with any certainty. Governments may introduce policies to combat inflation or unemployment: they do not have the

power to achieve a particular level of either. As we saw clearly in
Chapters 1 and 2, outside forces can knock a government off course:
exogenous shocks can have a critical impact. But economics, for all its
attempts at mathematical precision in analysis, is an imperfect science.
Not enough is known about, for example, the way inflation is trans-
mitted within an economy to be able to target it with any degree of
certainty or accuracy. Economies change constantly: what seemed like
a sure recipe for bringing down unemployment may no longer seem
effective. Economists may even be unsure of exactly what has changed
and why – which makes reformulating policy difficult. So governments and public policy-makers face enormous problems in trying to
develop effective policies.

In spite of the political rhetoric of a parliamentary democracy, it is
rare for a policy to be overturned completely, or to be reversed. Most
governments share fundamentally similar economic objectives; in the
second half of the twentieth century the aim was constantly to improve
living standards for as many people as possible. Of course, successive
governments may disagree about the best means of achieving this
objective. But none has publicly endorsed inflation, no Prime Minister
wants to see unemployment rise, no politician actively canvasses the
idea of falling standards in schools or hospitals. There are different
levels of tolerance for some of these things, it is true, and different
views about what can be done to affect them in the short run. But these
differences underline the inexact nature of economics and economic
policy; politicians – and some economists – may like to sound as if
they are certain, but no one can be.

Policy in most areas is tinkered with at the edges rather than
overhauled, although there are, of course, plenty of examples of radical
tinkering. Take the first budget of the Thatcher government in 1979.
Most commentators were shocked when the government, only six
weeks in office, slashed the level of income taxes and virtually doubled
the standard rate of VAT. This was indeed a radical step. It clearly had
an impact on the way people behaved with their money: they could
keep far more of what they earned before tax, and there was an
incentive for them to think more carefully about spending decisions
because of the much higher rate of sales tax. Inflation went up as a
result of the VAT rise. There is no clear agreement, however, on what
the impact of these changes was on people's behaviour. And when
looked at closely, this was less radical a step than it first appears. These
changes did not, for example, reduce the size of either the public sector

or the tax burden: they merely altered the way the revenue needed for government spending was raised.

In fact, the government would have found it difficult to do much in the short term with the relative share of the economy accounted for by the public sector. Most public spending, even now, is committed long in advance. The state has to pay benefits to large groups of people – the unemployed, the poor, the elderly, the sick and disabled. It cannot stop making these payments. Another large portion goes on the salaries of government workers. The government cannot just sack people to save money: just like any other employer, it has legal obligations to its employees. A large proportion of government spending in any financial year is already committed and cannot be altered in the short term.

So policy-makers have their hands tied. They can set about changing the policies of their predecessors but they can usually do so only slowly, a bit at a time. In 1997, when Labour regained power, the new Chancellor, Gordon Brown, was radical: he gave responsibility for setting interest rates to the Bank of England, catching everyone (including the Bank) by surprise. But he did not alter the inflation target he had inherited from his Conservative predecessor, nor did he alter the broad approach to controlling inflation, by setting a specific target.

The uncertainty factor

There is another reason for a relatively slow pace of change in economic policy. We have already seen that economics is an inexact science. One of the reasons for this is that it cannot be studied in laboratory conditions. It is impossible to take account of all the things going on in an economy when trying to decide which policies are more effective than others in achieving certain objectives – all the factors under scrutiny are constantly in flux and often unpredictable both in their behaviour and in their impact. Cutting interest rates, for instance, should provide a stimulus to economic growth; encourage industrial investment; and weaken the exchange rate, making it easier to export goods. But businesses may hold back on investment plans if they think interest rates are going to fall further. And a cut in UK interest rates may not bring about a fall in the value of the pound if other countries

Box 3.1   Forecasting

Economic forecasting is now a highly sophisticated econometric process, but that does not stop forecasters getting it wrong. Besides the Treasury's own forecast, which is revised far more often than it is published, there are several other elaborate computer models trying to predict what will happen to the UK economy (including those of the National Institute for Economic and Social Research, the London Business School and the Ernst and Young ITEM Club, which uses the Treasury's own model but comes up with different answers). The various forecasts sometimes, but not always, agree on the general trend of the economy, but they rarely agree on anything more specific.

Sometimes all the forecasts are wrong. For example, virtually no one predicted that the economy would recover and inflation remain subdued after the pound's exit from the ERM in 1992. Sometimes a forecast can be spectacularly wrong: the Treasury persistently underestimated the path of inflation during 1988.

Why do the forecasters so often get it wrong? Part of the answer lies in the insufficiently accurate information about what is happening in the present. Feed in the wrong data and you get out wrong answers. But part of the explanation lies in the nature of forecasting itself. Models which try to predict the future are constructed using known economic relationships: they make assumptions about the link between indicators such as prices, earnings and unemployment. These assumptions are based in turn on observations about what has happened in the past. It is exactly like weather forecasting: a prediction of rain tomorrow is based on information showing that rain is most likely to follow the weather patterns prevailing today. Difficulties arise if these relationships change – models cannot easily take account of this.

Forecasts are anyway not meant to be exact predictions about the future, but measures of the probability of something happening. This is most easily seen in the way the Bank of England forecasts inflation. It presents a range of possible outcomes and gives the likely probability of each actually happening. Thus it can say where inflation is most likely to be at a given point in the future and show how great it believes is the likelihood that it will be higher or lower than that.

None of this helps policy-makers, who have to take account of forecasts when trying to shape policy. There is now a greater appreciation of the dangers of relying too heavily on one specific forecast. And alternative ways of trying to assess future economic trends, such as chaos theory, have begun to be explored. For the time being, however, policy-makers have to use their judgement as well as the forecasts they receive.

are cutting their interest rates by the same or more. It is a bold policy-maker who is convinced that any particular policy is guaranteed to bring about a specific result.

Experimentation in economic policy is therefore a risky business. If existing policies are seriously failing, boldness may be justified; certainty about the outcome can never be. Moreover, unlike a chemist or a physicist working in a laboratory, the experiment cannot easily be halted if things go awry. And there is no opportunity for a re-run. A chemist can repeat the same experiment in controlled conditions many times over. The economic policy-maker cannot: everything will be different and different in an uncontrollable way. A policy for bringing down unemployment may have spectacular results in the US; it will not be possible to replicate that policy exactly in Britain, which is a very different economy both in size and in its characteristics.

The policy process

So far, we have tended to focus on policy as something on which governments and policy-makers take the initiative. In fact, this is relatively rare. Of course, new governments come into office with a manifesto and a desire to be different from their predecessors. Even re-elected governments like to have new policy initiatives to boast about. But these will invariably be directed at relatively small areas of economic life. No policy-maker can hope to have an impact on everything all at once.

For policy-makers, it is a particularly unpalatable fact of economic life that most policy is inevitably *reactive*. However well intentioned policies may be, however carefully they have been prepared, governments invariably find themselves reacting to events that they had not and could not have foreseen. Lots of people have to do this every day: an airline pilot, for instance, has to be able to take split-second decisions in order to be able to respond safely and effectively to emergencies. But an airline pilot trains in a flight simulator before handling the real thing: policy-makers cannot do that. The best they can hope to do is learn by their and others' mistakes – something they are surprisingly bad at doing. So policy-makers tend to find themselves reacting to developments they had not anticipated – either from outside (exogenous shocks) or which result directly from the implementation of their policies.

The principal actors

Whether a policy is the result of an initiative or is reactive, the main actors in the process are the same (though their roles may be different). To understand the policy process, it is necessary to understand who is involved, and how. It is important to remember that this process is unique to Britain. Theories of public administration and public policy-making may provide some general laws about which groups in society influence policy and how, but each country has its own framework of government, its own processes which determine how policy is made.

The UK is, of course, a parliamentary democracy, with the executive arm of government deriving its power from its majority in the House of Commons. The policy-making process, therefore, revolves around the executive. The executive is not the source of all policy initiatives, as we shall see, nor is it the only source of pressure for reactive policy-making. It may not always get its way (see below, page 67). But in terms of the implementation of policy it is the *sine qua non*; if the executive arm is opposed to a policy there is virtually no chance of it being implemented.

The executive, however, is itself a composite: within it there is a whole range of actors who each have different interests and aims. How policy is made, and what policies emerge from the process, depend crucially on the relationship between these actors. A further complicating factor is that these relationships are not stable; they change over time, sometimes very substantially and very rapidly.

The Prime Minister

Clearly, the single most important person in this set of relationships is the Prime Minister. The Prime Minister is First Lord of the Treasury, a title which most Prime Ministers take quite seriously and which provides a powerful reminder of the relationship between the Prime Minister and the Chancellor of the Exchequer. The Prime Minister may not take any day-to-day interest in the management of the Treasury, but he or she certainly takes a very keen interest in economic policy. This goes back to what we noted earlier about the impact of economic policy: it is wide-ranging, affecting every aspect of daily life, and numerous studies have shown that it is crucial in determining the electoral success of governments as well as the approval ratings for governments in office. No government and no Prime Minister can afford to ignore policy-making in this area.

We have also noted, however, that the Prime Minister is technically only first among equals in the British system of government. In theory, he or she must secure the approval of the Cabinet to implement policy. In practice, this rule is not so clear-cut as it may seem. In the first place, Prime Ministers can always replace dissident ministers, provided that they can retain the confidence of the Cabinet and the party which they lead. This – like most of the policy-making process – is a matter of political judgement rather than mechanical rules. But often, especially with sensitive economic policy issues, the Cabinet is bypassed altogether. Decisions on sensitive issues such as monetary policy, the exchange rate and the contents of the budget will rarely – if ever – come before Cabinet. It is almost as rare for Cabinet members to find this objectionable.

When the Prime Minister or Chancellor needs political backing for a controversial policy, however, they are likely to seek explicit Cabinet approval. As described in the previous chapter, in late 1976 the Callaghan government was forced to apply for a large loan from the IMF to help with a large and growing balance-of-payments deficit; as a condition of the loan the IMF insisted on substantial cuts in government spending and borrowing – anathema to many members of the Labour government. The Prime Minister (James Callaghan) chaired a long series of Cabinet discussions to make sure he had the backing of a majority of his colleagues. Similarly in 1992, when sterling was forced out of the ERM, Prime Minister John Major involved some of his Cabinet colleagues in discussions about the crisis. He wanted some political support for the actions he and his Chancellor, Norman Lamont, were about to take. By contrast, when Margaret Thatcher finally decided to accept the recommendation of her Chancellor, John Major, that Britain join the ERM in 1990, most Cabinet ministers were not given any advance warning.

The Downing Street neighbours

Much the most important link in the process, then, is that between the Chancellor and the Prime Minister – Britain's most famous next-door neighbours. It is one of the most critical and difficult relationships in any government. There is a natural tension between the two. The Chancellor is in day-to-day control of the Treasury and of economic policy. He has access to the full range of Treasury information and advice. He is nominally responsible to both the Prime Minister and the Cabinet, and to Parliament, for the satisfactory conduct of economic policy, for sound management of the economy. He is ultimately responsible for collecting taxes, and customs and excise duties. Overall, it is a position of immense power.

But the Chancellor must at all times retain the confidence of the Prime Minister in what he is doing. The two are likely to have almost daily contact (there is a connecting corridor between Numbers 10 and 11 Downing Street). The Prime Minister will expect to be consulted about, or at least notified of, any important policy changes or initiatives. He or she will not welcome being presented with a *fait accompli* in an important area of policy, where there is no scope to insist on change before something is implemented. There are therefore very significant curbs on the Chancellor's putative power.

How much freedom the Chancellor has in practice to initiate and implement policy will depend on several factors. Most important is the political relationship between the Chancellor and Prime Minister. Is it a relationship of equals? Is the Chancellor someone to whom the Prime Minister owes favours? Does the Chancellor enjoy an important power base within the government which the Prime Minister must seek to accommodate? These issues will influence the outcome of any policy disagreement between the two.

Take the example of Margaret Thatcher and Nigel Lawson, her Chancellor between 1983 and 1989. During Lawson's time in the job, relations between the two deteriorated. As we saw in Chapter 2, Thatcher was furious when she discovered that the Chancellor had secretly been attempting to link sterling with the German mark in 1987–8: his aim had been to keep the level at three marks to the pound. But the Prime Minister felt unable to move against Lawson because of the critical role he had played in the general election victory in 1987 and because of her powerful public endorsements of him after the election. The relationship between the two became even worse during the summer of 1989, when Lawson and the Foreign Secretary, Sir Geoffrey Howe, tried to force Thatcher to make a stronger commitment to join the ERM. Shortly afterwards, Thatcher demoted Howe; but she felt unable to move against her Chancellor. The economic situation had become difficult with inflation and interest rates rising sharply, and the Prime Minister did not want to undermine confidence in her government's economic policy still further.

In the event, Lawson resigned voluntarily in October 1989, following yet another disagreement with Thatcher. Ironically, this significantly increased the influence of his successor as Chancellor, John Major. Although the new Chancellor was far less experienced than Lawson and, moreover, a relatively junior member of the government (although he was briefly Foreign Secretary before his appointment), Thatcher herself was now more vulnerable: she could not afford to lose two Chancellors without seriously undermining her own authority. She could certainly not afford to lose two Chancellors over the same fundamental issue, the ERM: in 1990, she finally accepted Major's recommendation that the UK join.

A close relationship – but not too close

After a year as Chancellor, Major succeeded Thatcher as Prime Minister. He still had much to learn about the nature of the relationship between the two offices. As Prime Minister he failed to see the need to use his Chancellor to dissociate himself from economic failure. When the UK was forced out of the ERM in 1990, Major loyally refused to dismiss Norman Lamont, his Chancellor. Lamont was not the instigator of the government's ERM policy; he had merely inherited the policy he was obliged to defend in very difficult circumstances. But replacing Lamont might have helped restore Major's political authority, something the Prime Minister never managed to regain.

More recently, the Labour government elected in 1997 demonstrated the power a Chancellor can acquire if he has what is regarded as a separate power base within the government. The relationship between the new Prime Minister, Tony Blair, and his Chancellor, Gordon Brown, was complex. Following the death of the Labour Party leader, John Smith, in 1994, Brown had plans to be a candidate for the leadership. In the event, however, he stood aside in favour of Blair. There was no evidence of substantive policy disagreement between the two men. Even so, in the early years of the new government, Brown appeared to have an unusual degree of freedom in formulating economic policy. This is widely assumed to be part of an implicit deal struck between the two following the 1994 leadership contest. But it also reflected Blair's recognition that the Chancellor had influential

supporters within the government and within Parliament, whose interests needed to be fully taken into account.

The Treasury

These, then, are the key political actors, the people who are ultimately
responsible for policy. But Chancellors and Prime Ministers do not act
alone, in isolation. They use officials and advisers, who are commonly
thought of as acting on the instructions of their political masters. In
fact, these officials have a great deal of power themselves both in
implementing policies and, more importantly, in formulating and initiating policies. The Treasury, the main government department for
which the Chancellor is responsible (the others are the Inland Revenue
and Customs and Excise), is a uniquely powerful institution within
government. Its role is a wide one: it is responsible for macroeconomic
policy; for the management and control of public spending; for the
overall direction of monetary policy; for management of the exchange
rate; and for supervision of large areas of microeconomic policy.

The Treasury's power derives partly from the breadth of its responsibilities; partly from the relative power of the Chancellor within the
political machine; partly from its ultimate control of public spending;
and partly from its access to information. Almost no aspect of government is outside the Treasury's purview. Every activity of government
and policy-making costs money: the Treasury's approval is technically
required in every instance. Of course, in practice, the Treasury's principal control of spending is at a more general level: government
ministers and their departments get approval for spending in large
blocs – they do not have to seek Treasury approval for each pound they
spend. And, technically, it is the Cabinet as a whole which approves
government spending plans. But this only strengthens the Treasury's
hand. The Chancellor and the Chief Secretary (a Cabinet minister and
number two in the Treasury) propose a total package for government
spending which it is difficult for other ministers to argue against:
within that total individual ministers must argue their case with the
Treasury. They have little incentive to support each other since, by this
stage, it is a zero-sum game – one spending minister's gain is another's
loss. (See Chapter 9 for a fuller analysis of public spending.)

Although much economic information is in the public domain, the
Treasury has privileged access to many official statistics before they

Box 3.2 Outside advisers

Chancellors and other Treasury ministers have long made use of special advisers, who are outside the normal machinery of government. They find it helpful to have someone able to bring a different perspective to economic policy and who is not constrained in the way in which government officials are. The use of these advisers has increased significantly since the early 1980s, and in particular since the election of the Labour government in 1997. Such advisers can be informal – one or two complete outsiders whom the Chancellor might talk to occasionally to sound out ideas. Or they may be special advisers, who become part of the government machine, with an office in the Treasury, a salary and a contract which obliges them to resign on the day their minister leaves office.

Advisers play two roles. First, they can think the unthinkable: come up with ideas or solutions to problems which may be unorthodox and which civil servants have either not thought of or have discarded as impracticable. Such ideas often *are* impracticable, but they can help stimulate the internal policy debate and generate other, more feasible ideas. In some cases, advisers may represent a particular economic philosophy which is not taken seriously within the official Treasury.

Advisers are also used by ministers to help ensure that civil servants do not impose too many policy constraints – perhaps by telling ministers that some favoured solution is unworkable. This function tends to be particularly important after a change of government, when new ministers are at their most suspicious of civil servants. Some politicians find it hard to believe that the civil service, having implemented the policies of the previous government, will be able to endorse and take an objective approach to very different policies. Ministers look to their special advisers to ensure that officials are not deliberately obstructive.

There is some evidence to suggest that the Blair government's use of outside advisers was greater than that of its predecessors. Certainly from 1997 there were more of them and they appeared to have a more central role, both in the Treasury and elsewhere.

are published by the Office for National Statistics (formerly the Central Statistical Office). It also has access to data never published – such as the amount of reserves used in supporting the exchange rate. And though the Treasury does publish forecasts of economic performance, it also prepares secret forecasts of economic indicators such as unemployment. Both these factors make it far more difficult for anyone –

inside and outside the government machine – to marshal arguments against Treasury policies.

Powerful but not omnipotent

More difficult, but not impossible. Other government departments do have some ability to influence economic policy and even in some cases to initiate it. Several ministries have a direct, sometimes the lead, role in important areas of economic policy. The Department for Education and Employment (DfEE) is in charge of schools, colleges and universities as well as employment policy; the Department of Trade and Industry looks after important issues such as competition policy; the Department for Environment, Transport and the Regions has wide-ranging economic responsibilities. But the crucial difference between these departments and the Treasury is the extent to which they derive power from the political influence of their ministers. The Treasury is a powerful department in its own right. It is represented at both official and ministerial level on every interdepartmental committee (known as Cabinet committees) which has any interest in economic policy. It is in charge of the annual public spending process (see Chapter 9). The Treasury can use its knowledge of economic developments both to initiate policy and to draw up reactive policies affecting the whole government machine. Other government departments, by contrast, depend heavily on their own minister's position within the government. A strong minister, with the ear of the Prime Minister or a separate power base whose support is important for the smooth running of the government, will make it easier for his or her department to stand up to and resist the Treasury. Weak ministers will be despised by their departments because they will lose more battles with the Treasury than they win.

The Old Lady of Threadneedle Street

The Bank of England is not technically a government department. But it plays an important part in the economic policy process, a role that was considerably enhanced in May 1997 when the Bank was made independent of the political process. It now has direct responsibility for key aspects of monetary policy, in particular the setting of interest rates. Previously the Bank had been intimately involved in the process of controlling inflation over a long period, covering many different approaches to counter-inflationary policy. Specifically, it had always been the Bank which announced any change in interest rates but, until 1997, it was the Chancellor (always in consultation with the Prime Minister) who actually decided on any change, after taking advice from the Bank and from Treasury officials.

Since 1997, the Bank – technically its Monetary Policy Committee (MPC) – has been responsible for setting interest rates. The Bank does not set the inflation target; it merely decides how best to meet it. The government's argument for introducing this change was to de-politicise interest rate policy, to remove it from the hands of politicians, and thus remove the temptation to tinker with interest rates – perhaps to cut them too soon or to delay raising them, depending on the electoral and political timetable. There was always the suspicion, for example, that Chancellors would try to avoid putting interest rates up too close to an election.

The other area of policy in which the Bank has a role is, of course, the exchange rate. This provides a clear illustration of the extent to which in the past the Bank's influence has been exercised in informal ways. Technically, the Bank acts as the Treasury's agent in managing the external value of the pound. If intervention in the foreign exchange markets is judged to be necessary, say, to halt a sharp decline in sterling, or to prevent it rising, the Bank will buy or sell pounds or foreign currencies to try to influence the markets. This is inevitably something of a hit-and-miss affair: markets rarely behave in the way governments would like, and Britain's foreign currency reserves are insufficient to intervene on a scale guaranteed to move the exchange rate in the right direction (this is true of most countries nowadays). Above all, the Bank is relying on its expertise, its much greater understanding of the financial markets, to achieve the government's objectives. This expertise, which the Bank has always made much of, has long been a powerful tool for the Bank to use when arguing its case within the government.

It has not, however, always ensured it won the argument. Some governments have been content to let the Bank intervene in the foreign exchange markets whenever it judged it necessary, although the more usual approach has been to set parameters within which the Bank could operate. Thus, for a period in the late 1970s, the Bank was expected to try to keep the pound somewhere around $1.77. When the

Thatcher government took office in 1979, however, the Bank lost all freedom of manoeuvre for a time: no intervention at all was permitted without the express sanction of Treasury ministers, who were ideologically opposed to the idea of government intervention in the foreign exchange markets.

The downside of informal influence

Influence which is informally acquired and exercised is a common feature of the British system of government (and many others). It reflects the imprecise way in which policy is inevitably formulated in democratic systems. But the Bank's experience also provides a useful reminder of how that influence – and indeed power – can be lost. Until recently, one of the most explicit powers enjoyed by the Bank had been the regulation of the banking sector – it supervised banks to make sure they were abiding by the rules and exercising due care with their depositors' money. The Bank continues to argue that it fulfilled this function well, that no system of supervision can prevent mishaps and that no financial transaction can be wholly risk free. But in the political and popular view, the Bank made serious mistakes. In 1984, it had to rescue Johnson Matthey Bank, at considerable cost to the taxpayer, in order to prevent panic in the banking system when JMB faced collapse. In 1991 depositors lost millions when the Bank of Credit and Commerce International was closed after proof that it was used for money laundering and had links with organised crime. And in 1995 one of Britain's oldest banks, Barings, collapsed when a futures trader in Singapore managed to evade bank supervisors in breaking the rules. Rightly or wrongly, the Bank's supervisory skills – its ability to spot trouble and protect depositors and shareholders – were called into question. In 1997 the new Labour government transferred responsibility for supervision to the new Financial Services Authority.

The Bank also used to act as the government's agent for the issuance of government debt, raising the money the government needed to borrow to balance its books, to make up the shortfall when tax revenues were lower than spending commitments. The aim was always (and still is) to secure the finest terms, that is, the lowest interest rates. This, too, was an important opportunity for the Bank to use its expertise to influence policy, for example by advising on the timing of government debt issues. Bank officials made much of their close links with the markets. But as part of the 1997 changes, responsibility for debt management was switched to the new Debt Management Office.

Parliament

So far we have said little about Parliament's role in economic policy. Technically both the House of Commons and the House of Lords have a part to play. Nearly all government policies must be approved by Parliament. (The House of Lords, though, has far more limited powers to upset government plans – since the Parliament Act of 1911, for example, it has been unable to delay financial legislation, and at most can only postpone the implementation of other legislative plans for two years.) In theory, both the Lords and the Commons can vote against government plans. In practice this is rare, since the executive branch of government has to have a majority in the Commons: in most cases a majority vote against government policy would be tantamount to a warning that the government could not survive in office.

On occasion, however, MPs can flex their parliamentary muscles. In 1994 the House of Commons voted against the Chancellor's budget plans to raise VAT on fuel from 8 per cent to 17.5 per cent. Some of the Conservative government's own MPs voted against the plan, and the Chancellor, Kenneth Clarke, was forced to find an alternative source of revenue to balance the books. It is worth noting, however, that this is very much a negative exercise of power: there are no recent examples of the House of Commons successfully initiating economic policy to which the government of the day was opposed.

Non-institutional actors

Besides the institutional actors – those people and bodies that have some sort of formal role in economic policy – many other actors influence the formulation of economic policy. These and the extent of their influence vary over time, and depend in part on the domestic and international contexts. There is an important distinction between those who seek to influence policy and those who succeed. Each year, the Chancellor receives a large number of submissions ahead of the annual budget: each seeks to argue the case for one or more changes which the supplicants believe to be desirable. But few of these submissions will carry much weight in the corridors of the Treasury. Most are, in a sense, seeking special favours and dispensations. There is no reason why an interest group seeking to further its interests should have a disproportionate influence on policy: it is the Chancellor's job, in theory, to take account of the wider public interest when framing policy.

Occasionally, a submission may carry some influence if it deals with the impact of a specific measure, perhaps an unintended and incidental result of a policy introduced for quite different purposes. (These usually relate to tax changes and are often obscure issues related to the taxation of companies). But a more important factor in determining the impact of such submissions will be their source. Bodies whose support is perhaps crucial to the government – such as the TUC or the Confederation of British Industry – may carry weight. Their recommendations on policy may not be accepted, but they are likely to be taken into account. Measuring the extent of such influence is clearly very difficult, however.

There have nevertheless been times when non-governmental bodies have played an important role in policy. During the Labour governments of Harold Wilson and James Callaghan between 1974 and 1979, for example, the trade unions, via the TUC, had an influential role in economic policy. The so-called Social Contract between the Labour Party and the unions promised policies helpful to workers in return for (rather vague) promises from the TUC to co-operate in the fight against inflation. The unions had played a less welcome role during the Heath government when they actively – and successfully – sought to undermine the government's economic policies – on both industrial relations legislation and counter-inflationary strategy.

The markets

More recently other external factors have come to the fore: in particular the 'markets'. This is a term loosely used to mean the international financial markets and in particular the foreign exchange markets. Even in 1967, Prime Minister Harold Wilson blamed the 'gnomes of Zurich' (a reference to Swiss bankers, but by which he really meant the international financial markets) for the forced devaluation of the pound. But the advent of floating exchange rates since the 1970s has made every national economy more vulnerable to changes in market sentiment –

which can occur very rapidly. In theory, the foreign exchange markets make technical adjustments in rates to reflect fundamental changes in one economy relative to another; in practice their behaviour is far more complex. Much has been written (none of it conclusive) about the 'herd' instinct of markets and their tendency to overshoot in one direction or another. Sentiment about a currency tends to sweep everyone in the same direction: if the majority of dealers suddenly lose confidence in a currency and start to sell their holdings of it, that will lead to a run on the currency – its value will fall sharply because far more people want to sell than buy it. For policy-makers, the end result is that markets can act in an unpredictable manner, which can seriously undermine policy objectives. In some cases the market response is so severe that remedial action is forced on a government.

Examples abound. In June 1972, the pound was forced out of the European snake – an arrangement to keep European currencies linked to each other – after only six weeks. The cost of defending the exchange rate to which the UK was committed became prohibitively high: $2.6 billion dollars from the country's foreign exchange reserves was spent on buying pounds to try to prop up the rate before the government gave up the attempt. In January 1985, sterling fell sharply against a surging dollar, partly because of a (mistaken) belief in the markets that the government was willing to see the pound's value decline. As the slide accelerated, ministers became alarmed and were forced to take action to persuade dealers and investors to start buying pounds: they did this by raising interest rates so that holding sterling became more attractive. The panic was such, however, that rates had to be increased by 3.5 percentage points before the fall was stopped. Yet there was little domestic justification for such a swingeing increase in borrowing costs. And as we saw in Chapter 2, in September 1992, the Major government faced a huge crisis with far-reaching political implications when the markets made it impossible for sterling to remain within the ERM. Dealers sold sterling in unprecedented amounts, all of which had to be exchanged for the rate prevailing within the ERM. Within hours it became clear that the UK did not have sufficient foreign exchange reserves to carry on meeting this obligation; and attempts to halt the run on sterling by raising interest rates (by 5 percentage points during one day) had no effect. Whether the judgements of the markets are right or not, their behaviour is something governments are obliged to take into account when formulating economic policy.

International obligations

Of course, the international financial markets do not represent the only external policy constraint. The UK has international obligations and commitments which also affect policy. Membership of the IMF is one: among other benefits, IMF membership brings the entitlement to temporary balance-of-payments assistance in the event of difficulty (see page 3). But as one of the shareholders of the IMF, and of its sister organisation, the World Bank, the UK has to put up its share of the capital which these bodies need to function. IMF membership can sometimes be uncomfortable, since the IMF regularly expresses its views on the economic policies of its members, including Britain. Unfavourable comment from the Fund is potentially serious – it could, for instance, trigger an unwelcome reaction from the foreign exchange markets.

The UK is also a founder member of the OECD. This is, more than anything, a forum for the exchange of views and information among the industrial country membership. But the OECD too can affect Britain's international standing, and the stability of the pound, by its comments on the outlook for the economy.

Europe

By far the most important international economic relationship the UK now has, however, is membership of the EU. There is now almost no aspect of British economic life which does not have an EU dimension. British officials and ministers spend a great deal of time in EU meetings, commuting endlessly between London and Brussels, Luxembourg and Strasbourg (the three cities where most day-to-day EU business is conducted). It would be difficult to overestimate the impact of the EU on British economic policy. The development of policies aimed at the free movement of labour, goods and capital within Europe clearly affects the UK's domestic economic policies in many and significant ways. The UK's international trade policy is now largely determined by the EU, for instance. Employment policy, competition policy, the financial services industry and policy affecting it are all closely bound up by EU rules. EMU – the move to a single European currency – which took effect in January 1999, also had a major impact on the British economy and British economic policy even though Britain decided against joining the first wave of EMU members.

The UK also has to contribute a large sum annually to the EU budget; it would have been a much larger sum had not the Thatcher government negotiated an automatic rebate arrangement in 1984. The rebate row dominated the UK's relations with the EU for a time in the 1980s, and had significant implications for its ability to influence other policies in the EU. (See Chapter 4 for a fuller discussion of European issues.)

The formal policy process

Large areas of economic policy are developed in an *ad hoc* way: there is no set procedure and no set timetable. Governments constantly find themselves having to respond to developments in the economy which warrant a new policy initiative or an adjustment to existing policy. But there are some annual cycles which provide a framework for policy development. The most well known of these is the annual budget cycle. Each year, the Chancellor goes to Parliament and sets out his plans for management of the economy and for taxation and spending. The budget is one the great set-piece occasions of British political life: it is followed closely by the public at large because it can have an immediate and clearly understood effect on people's financial welfare.

The exact nature of the process has altered several times over the past few years. For more than a hundred years, the budget was presented in the spring, usually March or April – essentially linked to the UK's fiscal year, which runs from April. The budget focused particularly on the revenue side of the government's plans. A more recent tradition was presentation of the government's spending plans during the preceding autumn – usually November – because of the longer lead time needed to implement changes in the coming year's spending plans. On each occasion, that is, twice a year, the Chancellor would precede the detail of his plans with a forecast for the economy, making clear that he based his spending and tax intentions on the Treasury's expectations for growth, inflation and other economic indicators.

In 1993, this format was changed: the Chancellor, Norman Lamont, announced that there would be one announcement linking taxation and spending, and that this would take place in November. He argued that it made sense to look at the two sides of the balance sheet together.

The change was short-lived: when the new Labour government took office in 1997, it introduced further refinements. At the time of writing there are two stages in the process: a so-called 'green' budget in November, which sets out the direction of the Chancellor's thinking but which contains no firm commitments; and a full budget, presented in March, when the Chancellor's plans are finalised – in theory after taking account of comments on his green budget. It is too soon to offer conclusions about the impact of this consultative process, though some critics have argued that the element of consultation is more apparent than real.

The Labour Chancellor, Gordon Brown, also introduced changes to the public spending cycle itself. He introduced a Comprehensive Spending Review to take place every three years: at the conclusion of each review plans for the following three years will then be fixed and not subject to annual review. The Review is overseen by the Chief Secretary and the Public Spending Committee of the Cabinet. The aim is to encourage individual spending ministers to look at the allocation of spending resources within their departments; to streamline responsibility for services when these are spread across departments; and to commit departments to achieving efficiency savings as part of their three-year spending allocation. The changes appear to strengthen the hand of the Treasury still further. The new arrangement abandons the previous rolling programme, whereby at each annual review a spending figure for the third year was added on. But it is too soon to say whether the new system will make a dramatic difference to the pattern of public spending as far as the overall total (as opposed to departmental totals) is concerned.

Even in a government strongly committed to cutting public spending, or at least cutting its rate of increase, it will be rare for ministers from spending departments not to seek more money from the Treasury. This is partly because they are likely to be convinced of the merits of the claims made by their department. Health ministers do not find it difficult to justify extra funds for the NHS; it is not their principal role to see the wider picture (though that is arguably their role as Cabinet ministers). There is also a political reward to be had for spending department ministers who squeeze extra resources from the Treasury: they gain respect within their department and they may also be seen as more effective operators (and as candidates for promotion) by the Prime Minister. These arguments can be expected to continue under the new Comprehensive Spending Review system.

The budget also provides the Chancellor with the chance to set out his overall macroeconomic strategy. He is, of course, free to adjust policy at any time: there are no legislative constraints on the government's ability to redirect its economic policy. This applies in theory to public spending plans as much as anything else: in the past, some Chancellors have changed their spending plans on several occasions outside the normal cycle. In the 1970s, Denis Healey, Labour Chancellor, became famous for his mini-budgets: there were nine of these in addition to the seven annual budgets presented between 1974 and 1979. Taxes can be changed as well, the only constraint being the administrative time needed to implement changes. In more recent times, however, the cycle for public spending and tax changes has been observed more rigorously: the Healey era is seen in retrospect as a time when the government often gave the appearance of lurching from crisis to crisis. Governments of both parties now take pride on their ability to stick with plans announced; and the Labour government which took office in 1997 has taken particular pride in its ability and determination to look to the longer term – hence the introduction of the Comprehensive Spending Review.

Policy for the long term

Increasingly, this long-term approach to economic management has become the norm in other areas of macroeconomic policy. As inflation has come down to levels comparable to those in other industrial economies during the 1990s, both the Conservative and now the Labour governments have worked to stick to a long-term target for inflation, announced annually, during the main budget speech. The Labour government's decision to give day-to-day control of monetary policy to the Bank of England was ostensibly aimed at strengthening this approach. Establishing a framework for stability became a central aim of all areas of economic policy in the 1990s (following the failure of earlier attempts during the 1980s). The more the government is able to stick to and deliver long-term policy objectives, it is argued, the more likely other actors in the economy will respond by adjusting their behaviour accordingly. Wage claims and investment decisions will both take account of the government's commitment to low inflation, for example. Clear and observed limits on the amount of public spending and the size of the public sector should create more opportunities for long-term investment in the private sector.

Stability may be a desirable objective, but it is difficult to achieve. No one has yet worked out how to prevent economies moving in cycles, with growth accelerating until a peak is reached, at which point the economy (i.e. GDP growth) begins to slow – until the process starts all over again. Governments tend to accept the cyclical nature of economies as a fact of life, though they have increasingly concentrated on trying to smooth out the fluctuations. The real problem arises when external shocks have a severe impact on the economy. The oil price rises of the 1970s; the stock market crash of 1987; the upward pressure on European interest rates following German reunification in 1990; the impact on the world economy of the Asian financial crisis of 1997–8; the Russian economic crisis of 1998: these all fed through in different ways to the British economy. In some cases, governments find it necessary to respond to such shocks by introducing immediate changes in policy. In 1987, the British government followed the practice of all the major economies in cutting interest rates to ensure that the world-wide collapse in share prices had less impact on economic activity than might otherwise have been the case. In other instances, governments may make it clear that they stand ready to act if developments else-where threaten to undermine their economic objectives.

Globalisation?

The close links between the domestic and the international economies are hardly new, as we saw in Chapter 1. There is an ongoing argument among academics about the significance of globalisation for economies in the twenty-first century. Some believe its impact is overstated, that the relationship between the national economy and the rest of the world is not that different from what it was thirty years ago; others argue that globalisation is becoming so entrenched that national govern-ments have less and less room for manoeuvre.

The truth probably lies somewhere in between. There are severe constraints now on the freedom governments have to set out and achieve policy objectives independently of the international economy. Business, for example, has become increasingly international in its approach: companies take a wide range of factors into account when making decisions about the location of their activity. Large multinational companies are now an economic force to be reckoned with. Governments know that high-wage, low-productivity economies will fare worse in the battle for investment. And cross-border investment is becoming more important than trade in driving international economic activity these days. So governments with heavily regulated labour markets find themselves forced to make a more explicit trade-off between jobs and job security for their citizens.

But these constraints were encountered by successive British governments for much of the twentieth century. The Labour government of 1949 did not want to devalue the pound: it was obliged to do so because of international obligations it had entered into. The Labour government of 1967 was equally unenthusiastic about the devaluation, for which it, too, could find no alternative. The Conservative government in 1973 could not ignore the impact of the oil price rises. The Major government of 1992 did not want to leave the ERM. The list is almost endless.

What governments seek to do therefore is influence developments in the international economy, with two objectives: to reduce the external constraints on their domestic policy freedom; and to shift the global economy in the direction they would like to see it go. International economic policy is therefore an important element of policy-making. British governments have long been major players in the international economic arena, often 'punching above their weight'. As we noted in Chapter 1, Britain was one of the principal architects of the post-war international economic settlement, although it did not achieve all its objectives in the negotiations, and it did not have as much influence as it would have liked over the implementation of that settlement.

The UK's initial involvement in the Bretton Woods negotiations, however, stemmed from the country's pre-war position as a major global power. The relative decline of the UK economy since the war has meant that disproportionate British influence (where it has been exercised) has increasingly been derived from the experience, expertise and general diplomatic skills of officials and ministers. The close diplomatic links between the US and Britain also helped. The UK is, of course, still one of the world's biggest economies and is represented in all the main international economic groupings, including the G-7, which. while informal, still largely dictates global policy on finance and economics. Britons always have senior positions in the IMF, the World Bank, the World Trade Organisation, the EU and the OECD; Roy Jenkins was President of the European Commission 1977–81; a

British official became Secretary-General of the Commission in the 1980s; and in the late 1990s, British nationals headed the Bank for International Settlements and the European Investment Bank. The holders of such international positions are supposed to be neutral. But it is widely accepted that they will at least retain close links with their home governments; in international economic diplomacy such contacts and channels of communication can be important, if only by ensuring that a point of view is heard, if not accepted.

The policy process at the international level is even more complicated than at national level. It tends to be much more *ad hoc*, for a start; there is no annual cycle to be followed, however loosely. Progress on specific issues needs the agreement of far more people, whose interests are likely to be more diverse than any domestic group of policy-makers. Each party in a policy negotiation will in turn have conflicting interests to satisfy at home. Thus, for example, major decisions affecting the IMF – particularly those involving an increase in the Fund's resources – inevitably get stalled for prolonged periods while the executive branch of the US government persuades Congress to implement an agreement reached with other countries.

Over the years, the UK has been a remarkably successful player in this policy arena. British negotiators have usually managed to go further in achieving their aims than they might have expected given Britain's relative economic weight. The UK continues to hold a disproportionately high quota (which brings voting rights with it) in the IMF and the World Bank, for example. Britain has often been able to initiate policy developments both in the Bretton Woods organisations and in the G-7. In 1999, Chancellor Gordon Brown assumed the chair of the IMF's principal policy-making committee, a position which several other British Chancellors have held over the years. The one area where the UK appears significantly to have failed to achieve its objectives is in Europe: from the creation of the EEC, as it was then called, in 1957 right up to the launch of EMU, British policy on Europe has largely consisted of running to catch up (see Chapter 4).

The ideal and the attainable

The complexities of international economic policy bring into sharp relief the challenge all economic policy-makers seek to meet: to bridge the gap between the ideal and the attainable. Governments would like to provide their citizens with what those citizens want: low taxes, a high standard of public services, low unemployment, low or zero inflation, low interest rates for borrowers, high interest rates for depositors, a stable exchange rate which makes imports cheap and exports competitive. Some of these are more obviously in conflict than others. No one seriously thinks that two levels of interest rates are actually feasible, for instance. But in practice *most* of these objectives are incompatible with each other. The government can take any one goal and give that priority, and if it single-mindedly pursues that goal it can probably achieve it. But it could do so only at the expense of other objectives. It does not need a sophisticated grasp of economics to work this out. Take the commonly heard plea of business people, who want low interest rates in order to make investing and running their businesses easier and cheaper. If these businesses export, they usually also want a low exchange rate, which makes their goods more competitive abroad. But they also want low inflation. What should the government do? If it sets inflation as its principal target, it will have to raise interest rates if inflationary pressures grow too strong. That is likely to put upward pressure on the pound. At this point some business people shift their ground and say they do not mind a bit of inflation. What they want, they claim, is stable interest rates and a stable pound. But suppose then the government shifts its attention to sterling. Its main weapon then is the level of interest rates. Sterling might fall for reasons unconnected with British economy – other economies in Europe, for instance, might seem more attractive to the international investors who shift their money around every day. If this fall were severe enough, the Bank of England might take the view that the inflation target was at risk and raise interest rates to offset that threat. It is not hard to imagine that businesses would then vehemently complain about the pain being inflicted on them by government.

Economic policy, then, is a matter of trade-offs. As we have seen, the process at both the domestic and international level involves negotiation between parties with conflicting interests. The relative power of those parties will ultimately determine whose interests come to the fore and whose view holds sway. Policy-makers try to take account of these conflicts by constructing policies with the widest possible appeal. They do this both within the government machine – the Chancellor and his officials will try to pre-empt argument by ensuring the support of key policy-makers elsewhere – and outside; and at national and international levels. How they do this in relation to specific areas of economic policy is the concern of the chapters which follow.

4　British policy and the European Union

We saw in previous chapters that British economic policy cannot be made in a vacuum: the British economy is subject to, and policy must therefore respond to, a wide range of pressures related to developments outside the UK. Partly as a result of earlier policy decisions, policy-makers have less direct control than they used to over many of the actors, domestic and international, who affect the economy; they are vulnerable to the dictates of others. Individuals; corporations; financial institutions and markets; international organisations such as the IMF and the OECD; and other, often larger and more powerful economies: all have the capacity to influence policy, and to aid in or prevent the achievement of policy objectives. Both the introductory and thematic chapters of this book take account of these economic variables as far as possible.

Europe and supranationality

But the UK's relationship with the EU requires a separate chapter. In part, this is because of the complexities of the issues involved. Almost no aspect of British economic policy is untouched by the European dimension: both macro- and microeconomic policies are influenced or constrained to a considerable extent. But the principal reason for tackling the EU separately is that this is a fundamentally different kind of external policy constraint: the UK's relationship with the EU is qualitatively distinct from, say, that with the IMF because the EU is an explicitly supranational body.

This difference can seem a subtle one. If we take the economic crisis of 1976, for example, when the British government applied to the IMF for an emergency loan, a significant shift in policy was forced on the government: the IMF was willing to grant the funds only on

condition that policy shifts (large cuts in public spending and borrowing) took place. British economic freedoms were clearly constrained.
But the IMF had no power as such to force those policy changes: it
could merely withhold funds. The government did, at least in theory,
have alternatives: these may have seemed more painful but some
policy-makers were, at the time, advocating them.

The EU, by contrast, has explicit legal powers which override those
of the UK. These powers were given to what was then known as the
European Communities by the European Communities Act of 1972
and other subsequent legislation passed by the British Parliament.
These are specified and limited: the EU cannot dictate the whole of the
UK's economic policy. But in the areas where legal authority has been
ceded, the EU's powers are substantial.

In the first place, the UK has, like all member states, to make a
financial contribution to the EU budget. The UK has always been one
of the larger contributors to the budget, and the size of the British
contribution came to be one of the most controversial aspects of
membership, both in Britain and in the rest of the EU (see below,
pages 88–90). But membership imposes other constraints on British
policy-makers. The government, for instance, can be prevented from
giving financial aid to save state-run businesses (as well as those in the
private sector); the UK has no individual negotiating authority in
international trade negotiations; the level of payments British farmers
receive is decided by the EU. In disputes in any of the relevant areas,
Britain must abide by rulings of the European Court of Justice. It is
important to remember that these 'restrictions' apply to every member
state and that the UK freely entered into these arrangements. That does
not lessen the impact which EU membership has on policy formulation
and execution. It is also important to remember that in no other EU
country is EU membership so politically contentious. This, too, has a
direct bearing on the economic policy process.

The UK and Europe: a brief history

We saw in Chapter 1 that the UK initially decided against involvement
in the developments that led to the modern EU. For much of the post-
war period the focus was on the relationship with the US and, to a
diminishing extent, the Commonwealth. The issue of British membership has never ceased to be contentious. A combination of domestic

pressures and, far more importantly, the perception that the UK's foreign and economic interests were different from those of continental Europe led the UK to abstain from discussions about, and the subsequent formation of, the ECSC in 1951. Similarly, under a different government, the UK chose not to become seriously involved in the process which led to the signing of the Treaty of Rome in 1957, which paved the way for the establishment of the EEC on 1 January 1958. (The founding members of both institutions were Belgium, France, Germany, Italy, Luxembourg and the Netherlands.) Middle-ranking British officials attended the early EEC negotiations but were withdrawn before the process was complete.

For as long as British policy-makers took the view that the UK's foreign policy and economic interests differed from those of mainland Europe, they tended to see little point in joining. But when these views changed, and the UK sought to join, the welcome was not as warm as might have been expected. Negotiations in the early 1960s, initiated by the Conservative government led by Harold Macmillan, were aborted when the French President, Charles de Gaulle, suddenly vetoed the British application in January 1963. He repeated this tactic in November 1967, when Harold Wilson's Labour government sought to join. By the time Edward Heath's Conservative government won power in 1970, de Gaulle had resigned as French President and a new application was made to join. The negotiations were successfully concluded in early 1972, and the UK joined the European Communities (including the EEC) on 1 January 1973. Ireland and Denmark, both with strong economic ties to the UK, joined at the same time. (Greece joined in 1981, Spain and Portugal in 1986, and Austria, Finland and Sweden in 1995.)

When Labour regained power in 1974, it did so after having opposed the decision to join, and having committed itself to a 'fundamental renegotiation of the terms of entry'. In the event, the 'renegotiations', largely cosmetic, enabled the government to announce it had achieved improved terms, of which it recommended acceptance in a referendum in 1975. Successive governments have been more or less committed to membership, often not enthusiastically, and frequently struggling to contain divisions about Europe within their party. The Conservative governments of Margaret Thatcher and John Major saw these divisions grow to uncontrollable levels by the late 1990s. In the 1980s, the opposition Labour Party was again officially committed to withdrawal for a significant period, but by the end of the 1990s the Labour government of Tony Blair was, in theory at least, wholeheartedly committed to playing a positive role within the EU. Blair was also in favour in principle of the UK ultimately joining the process of EMU. The Conservative opposition was by now far more sceptical of the benefits of membership of the EU, and vehemently opposed to joining EMU – the official line was to rule out EMU until at least 2007.

These domestic arguments, visible to the UK's fellow members, have had an important influence both on EU policy and on the UK's own economic policy-making. To understand this more clearly, it is important first to get an idea of how the EU's own policy-making process works.

The structure of the EU

From its inception in 1958, the EEC co-existed with the ECSC and the European Atomic Energy Community (Euratom). In 1987, these Communities became the European Community when the European Single Act came into force. When the Maastricht Treaty (the Treaty on European Union) came into effect, on 1 November 1993, the name changed again, to the European Union. All agreements affecting the EU are technically amendments to the Treaty of Rome, which still therefore forms the legal basis for the EU's existence. A mass of legal detail provides the framework for the structure of the EU, establishing the various policy-making and executive bodies and spelling out exactly what the competence of these bodies is – in determining where the EU has a say in or control of national policy.

The central policy-making body is the Council of Ministers: one from each member state. Normally these are foreign ministers, but other groups of ministers meet regularly – economic and finance ministers, agriculture ministers, trade ministers and so on. Heads of government meet together at the European Council at least twice a year, often more frequently. They make decisions on the most important or contentious issues.

A huge array of committees of officials, usually shadowing and preparing the ground for ministerial councils, meet frequently; national officials commute endlessly between their home countries and Brussels, Luxembourg and Strasbourg, the sites of most EU business. One of the key groupings is COREPER – the Committee of Permanent Representatives (the member states' national ambassadors to the EU) and their subordinates.

The European Commission is the EU's civil service, although it operates very differently from the British civil service. The Commission itself comprises twenty separate Commissioners: a President and then nineteen others who have individual directorates-general for which they are responsible. The Commissioners are also collectively responsible for the Commission's functioning and its policy proposals. Each Commissioner is nominated by a member state: smaller states have one, the larger states (the UK, France, Germany, Italy and Spain) have two. The Commission is a large bureaucracy (based mainly in Brussels but with officials in Luxembourg) and it is not limited to executive responsibilities. It also has the power (and uses it) to initiate policy, though such initiatives must then be approved by the Council of Ministers.

There is also a European Parliament (based mainly in Strasbourg), which started out as a non-representative Assembly but which has seen its powers strengthened considerably over the years. It is now directly elected throughout the EU, using a system of proportional representation. The Parliament's powers are still somewhat limited relative to the Council of Ministers and to the Commission, but these powers increased significantly during the 1990s. For example, it can vet (and veto) the appointment of Commissioners, and in certain instances force the resignation of the entire Commission, as it did in March 1999.

The European Court of Justice, although not one of the most prominent of EU institutions, is extremely powerful. It is the final arbiter of any dispute about the various EU Treaties, and it is therefore in a position significantly to influence the business of the EU. The European Court of Auditors also has extensive powers: its job is to try to ensure that EU money is properly spent. The European Investment Bank (EIB) is the world's largest lender and is also one of the institutions set up under the Treaty of Rome. Member states are shareholders in the Bank, which operates inside and outside the EU.

The EU policy process

Contact between London and Brussels (and Luxembourg and Strasbourg) is incessant: ministers and officials meet every day in one forum or another. There are also frequent meetings in other European cities, as well as a never-ending round of bilateral contacts between national governments. This is all part of the normal policy-making process. The extent of these contacts is a reminder of the degree to which British policy is inextricably linked to and in some cases governed by EU policy, and therefore of the significance of the EU in terms of achieving British economic policy objectives. It is this relationship which is most directly and importantly affected by the somewhat ambivalent British attitude to the EU. This is because of the ways in which policy emerges from the various bodies of the EU and the large number of meetings involved.

The key is the Council of Ministers, to which, ultimately, all important policy issues go; and in particular the methods used to reach agreement. For many of the most crucial decisions, unanimity is required: every member state must agree to Treaty amendments before they can take effect, for example. But achieving unanimity among fifteen states can be a difficult and time-consuming process, and so a system of qualified majority voting (QMV) operates, for an increasing number of important but ultimately second-rank policy issues. Voting is weighted to take some account of the huge gap between the largest and smallest member states, and to try to ensure that the big states are not dictated to by the small states. These population-based weightings are not precise.

While QMV is designed to avoid a group of large states being forced to accept decisions to which they are opposed, it also is intended to give groupings of small states some veto power. Clearly, in issues subject to QMV, no single member state has a veto. Any member opposed to a policy must therefore seek allies in order to be able to exercise a veto, or be prepared to accept losing the argument. Even where unanimity operates, no member will want to exercise its veto power too often, if it is the only state opposed to something. There is a risk that on a subsequent occasion another member may choose to exercise its veto on an issue which the first country is particularly keen to see approved.

It is not difficult to see that the policy-making process in the EU is very much one which involves a good deal of bargaining. No member state is going to achieve all its objectives all the time. The system is designed to ensure that vital national interests can be protected. But it can work only if the judgement of what constitutes vital national interest is carefully calculated, and the veto used sparingly. Achieving national policy objectives necessarily involves building alliances – with the Commission, other member states and, increasingly, the European Parliament. This is the only way to achieve positive policy successes – that is, getting a chosen policy objective endorsed or adopted by the EU. It is also the only way to achieve what might be called negative successes – preventing an unwelcome policy from going ahead – consistently over a long period.

One other aspect of the EU process is relevant here: the Presidency of the Council of Ministers. This rotates every six months, moving to each member state in turn (according to a somewhat complicated alphabetical formula). The Presidency confers no explicit advantage: there are no extra votes, no exemptions from the normal voting rules. But for the six months of the Presidency, that country is in the chair at every EU meeting. In a very real sense, the Presidency is able to exert influence to accelerate business it deems important. It is now the custom for many of the ministerial meetings and some meetings of officials to take place in the country holding the Presidency: there is always at least one European Council there. Although some countries handle their turn more effectively than others (it is easier for the larger countries to exploit), the opportunity to exert influence, though not specific power, over the EU's conduct of business is highly valued by them all.

It is possible in some senses to see the EU policy process as similar to that operating in the UK at the national level. We saw in Chapter 3 that policy outcomes are often the result of some kind of horse-trading between different parties. But there is a fundamental difference, insofar as the EU policy process infringes on national policy: the UK is only one of the bargaining parties involved, and may not – certainly will not on every occasion – succeed in meeting its objectives.

The areas of policy impact

As the momentum has continued towards closer co-operation and some degree of economic integration among EU member states, the areas of economic policy affected by the EU have been substantially extended. The EU now has involvement in foreign policy, crime, justice and immigration matters. But economic policy remains at the centre of the EU, where it is divided into those areas in which the European Commission has independent authority to act on behalf of the EU; and those areas in which policy is decided on by the Council of Ministers and executed by the Commission. In practice, of course, there is some overlap between the two. The most important areas where the Commission has wide powers in its own right are international trade negotiations (which it conducts on its own authority on member states' behalf) and competition policy within the EU (and therefore within member states).

Economic policy at the European level impinges on almost every conceivable area of British domestic policy – agriculture, employment, trade, transport, public spending, financial services and regulation, and general macroeconomic policy. It therefore represents an additional constraint which policy-makers have to take into account. Even those areas where the UK has negotiated the right not to become involved, such as the ERM in the 1980s, or EMU in the late 1990s, have had an enormous impact on both the content and the conduct of British policy.

The policy consequences of UK membership

It is, of course, impossible to be sure how British policy might have developed if the UK had not joined the EU. But some of the policy consequences of membership are clear. The UK would not have had a system like the Common Agricultural Policy (CAP) for rewarding its farmers. It would not have been subject to the EU requirements on tax harmonisation, which mean, for example, that VAT may not be set below 15 per cent. The UK may not have adopted a VAT system in the first place: doing so was a requirement of entry. British producers and consumers would not have had access to the European Single Market, which provides for the (relatively) free movement of goods, capital and labour within the EU. British citizens would not have been able freely to live anywhere in the EU and claim benefits on the same terms as nationals in the same way (and nor would other EU nationals have been able to settle in Britain on similar terms). All these are examples of the way British economic policy explicitly changed to accommodate British membership of the EU.

Because of the political doubts about membership, there have been endless arguments over the years over whether these policy changes were beneficial or detrimental. The arguments extend to the direct economic effects of membership. Did the UK grow faster or more slowly than it otherwise would as a consequence of being in a customs union and the Single European Market? Did the UK's net contribution to the EU budget deprive its public services of resources? Did British industry become more or less competitive as a result of the various policies operated by the EU which affect companies?

These issues go to the heart of many of the debates within the UK which preceded entry and in the run-up to the 1975 referendum. These focused on the potential dynamic benefits of membership, and were linked partly to the benefits of being in a customs union and free trade area as opposed to the costs of being outside. But they were also concerned with the potential benefits of matching the rates of economic growth which the six founding members had managed to achieve. The early 1970s were a period of considerable economic uncertainty and upheaval in the UK, as awareness grew of the extent to which it was falling sharply behind its continental European neighbours. Their growth rates, productivity improvements and general economic performance had generally exceeded those of the UK and the proponents of the dynamic benefits argument were convinced this improved performance derived from EEC membership. This argument appeared less convincing when, shortly after British accession, the European economies were all badly affected by the oil price shock and a combination of rising unemployment and inflation – what became known as 'Eurosclerosis' (see Chapter 1).

Nevertheless, it is clear that membership does have a strong impact on British economic performance, as well as on the British economic policy-making process itself. Trade disputes between the EU and other countries, for example, can affect British exports, jobs and thus economic growth. There were several such disputes between the EU and the US in the 1980s and 1990s. When disputes escalate to the extent that each side bans imports from the other, British goods can be affected. Yet responsibility for international trade negotiations lies with the European Commission rather individual member states. Member states can only seek to influence policy in this area. The Commission is unlikely to take a policy stance to which all or even most member states are opposed. But there is a significant risk that the UK will find itself in a policy dispute with a third country which it might have preferred to avoid. So the direct economic effects as well as the policy implications are important, and both bring us back to the policy process within the EU.

The consequences of British ambivalence

The UK has consistently held back from the most significant developments within the EU at every stage. As it was a late applicant and an even later entrant, the final accession negotiations obliged the UK to join the EEC largely as it was, rather than as it might have turned out with Britain as a founding and influential member. Not only did that mean that the UK had to accept both the CAP and the Common Fisheries Policy as they stood; it also led to the UK paying an inequitable level of contributions to the EEC. This caused one of the most damaging rows in the Community in the 1980s (see below). Britain decided against joining the ERM in 1979: when the pound eventually went in, in October 1990, it did so in inauspicious circumstances, and sterling was forced to leave two years later (see Chapters 5 and 8 for a full discussion). And when the final stage of EMU began in 1999, the UK had decided to wait and see before joining.

All these steps towards greater economic integration of the EU member states went ahead in spite of Britain's doubts. It is not possible, even with hindsight, to say what the impact on the British economy would have been had the UK been an enthusiastic participant. No one can know whether sterling would have survived in the ERM had the UK signed up in 1979. The arguments put forward at the time seemed to suggest the UK's best interest lay in the decision taken by policy-makers. This was true on many of the occasions when the UK decided to stand back from collective decisions taken by its European partners. But the cumulative impact of individual decisions created the impression of the UK as a reluctant partner in Europe: and the cumulative price was reduced influence on all aspects of European policy. The policy-making process in the UK does not always take this into account, or recognise the importance of linkage between issues. Responding negatively on one policy front may undermine the UK's ability to influence another policy, even though these two policy areas may be unrelated to each other. It may be that on any one issue the same British position would still be adopted once broader strategic questions had been considered, but that might not always be the case. The difficulty often faced by the UK is that ultimately it will have to abide by EU policies which apply to all members, but it might not have had as much influence in defining those policies as it would like.

The budget rebate

The arguments over the British budget contribution illustrate this well. By the time the UK joined the European Communities, much of its policy-making and financial structure had been long established. In particular, the CAP, which accounted for a large part of the Community's

Box 4.1   The UK and the EEC budget

Even during the original negotiations for the UK's accession to the EEC, it was recognised that the budgetary arrangements might result in it paying an unduly large amount to the EEC budget. It was agreed that if 'an unacceptable situation' arose, something would be done.

The Wilson government sought to renegotiate the terms of membership in 1974–5, but the extra provisions intended to take more account of the UK's relative economic position were so restrictive that they were never triggered. The problem remained when Margaret Thatcher became Prime Minister in 1979, by which time the UK was the second largest net contributor to the budget.

1980 net receipts from the EC budget (a minus sign signifies a net contribution)

	Net receipts (£million)	Per capita GDP (EC average = 100)
Belgium and Luxembourg	997	108
Denmark	188	111
France	48	116
Germany	-724	118
Ireland	289	61
Italy	491	77
Netherlands	193	105
United Kingdom	-1203	91

Data from W. Godley, 'The UK and the Community budget', in W. Wallace, ed., *Britain in Europe* (Heinemann, 1980).

Thatcher secured two rebate deals. The first, agreed in 1980, amounted to a refund of two-thirds of the British contribution; it lasted for only three years and was subject to annual adjustment. The second, agreed at the Fontainebleau Summit in 1984, was more permanent. It amounted to a rebate of two-thirds of what would otherwise have been the UK's net contribution. The rebate is financed equally by all member states except Germany, which, as the largest net contributor, pays only two-thirds of its normal contribution to the rebate. There have been subsequent attempts by other member states to re-open this rebate deal, but none has so far met with success.

budget, was already in place; so was the system for calculating member states' contributions to that budget. These arrangements penalised the UK in two ways. First, its agricultural sector was much smaller than that in most other member states. It therefore received less money from the CAP than other states. Second, the British economy was less closely linked to the rest of the EEC in terms of exports and imports; specifically, the UK imported more goods from countries outside Europe. Since contributions to the budget were at that time largely determined by excise duties imposed on such imports, the UK ended up paying proportionately more money into the European kitty. Taken together, these factors meant that the UK contributed far more to the budget than it got in receipts. Yet Britain was one of the poorer members of the Community, in terms of per capita GDP. Neither the transitional arrangements negotiated at the time of entry nor the re-negotiations conducted in 1974–5 had much impact on this problem. By the late 1970s, the UK's net payments to the EEC budget were soaring (see Box 4.1). Attempts to reduce these payments got nowhere.

When Margaret Thatcher became Prime Minister in 1979, she made resolving this problem a priority. Acrimonious negotiations, often at heads of government level, dragged on interminably. But a temporary deal agreed in 1980 was finally replaced with a permanent rebate arrangement negotiated at the Fontainebleau Summit in 1984. For the UK, this was ultimately highly successful: a net reduction in contributions and thus public expenditure of significant amounts. Thatcher's technique won her respect and admiration, but few friends within the Community. Moreover, it came with a price: as part of the deal, Thatcher signed up to the Single European Act, which gave a further push to European integration and was a move she later came to regret. Important issues were at stake for the British government in the budget negotiations and the UK had a strong case. But the arguments significantly weakened Thatcher's influence in other areas of policy. She was unable to halt or even slow progress towards EMU. By the end of the century, this had become the single most important influence on the British economy and economic policy-making.

EMU: *fait accompli*

By the time the UK joined the European Communities, a commitment to EMU was already in place. At that time it was planned to take effect

---

Box 4.2   Economic and Monetary Union

Plans for EMU among members of the EEC first surfaced with the Werner report in 1970, which envisaged the completion of EMU by 1980. The report was soon buried. But the creation of the EMS in 1979 (see Box 2.5 on page 48) provided advocates of EMU with another opportunity. In the mid-1980s, the momentum for EMU gradually built up and in 1988 a special committee was set up under the President of the Commission, Jacques Delors, to explore the options. The Delors report was completed in 1989 and discussed at the Madrid Summit that year. The Delors report provided the basis for the EMU plan which was eventually adopted. It envisaged a gradual approach to monetary union and it also recommended that participants should agree to fiscal constraints.

The final plan was adopted in the Treaty on European Union agreed at Maastricht in 1991. EMU would be in three stages:

Stage 1:   all prospective EMU members in the narrow bands of the ERM, with capital controls to be phased out;

Stage 2:   to start on 1 January 1994, with the creation of the European Monetary Institute, which was to prepare the ground for the new European Central Bank; national central banks to be made independent; and ERM realignments to take place only in exceptional circumstances;

Stage 3:   to start on 1 January 1997 if a majority of member states met the Maastricht criteria (see Box 4.5 on page 95); otherwise it would start automatically on 1 January 1999, with the countries which qualified. At this point exchange rates would be irrevocably fixed, the new currency (the euro) would come into effect and all national currencies (notes and coins) would be phased out within three years.

On 1 January 1999 eleven member states – Germany, France, Italy, the Netherlands, Belgium, Luxembourg, Spain, Portugal, Austria, Ireland and Finland – joined EMU. Greece (which did not qualify) is committed to joining at the earliest possible opportunity. The UK, Denmark and Sweden all qualified for entry but chose not to join.

---

by 1980, an objective abandoned in the mid-1970s. The EMS was established in 1979. The key component of this, the ERM, aimed to link participating currencies together (see Box 2.5 on page 48 for an explanation of how it worked) and this came to be seen as a first step to EMU and a single European currency. During the 1980s, British

---

Box 4.3   Crisis within the Exchange Rate Mechanism

From the UK's point of view, the ERM crisis erupted during 1992 and culminated in sterling's abrupt departure from the mechanism on 16 September. But from the broader European perspective, the crisis dragged on for much longer and threatened to wreck the plans for EMU.

The main source of the problem was the asymmetric shock suffered by the system following German reunification in 1990. For domestic reasons, the Bundesbank raised interest rates as part of the process of adjusting to the costs of unification. This forced other members (with the exception of Britain) to raise their rates too, in order to maintain the existing currency relationships within the ERM. During 1992 the foreign exchange markets became much more volatile following the vote against the Maastricht Treaty in the Danish referendum. Over the summer of 1992, speculative pressure gradually built up against sterling and the lira.

On 13 September, the lira was devalued by 7 per cent. On 16 September overwhelming pressure forced the British authorities to suspend membership of the ERM and the lira followed suit the day after. In November, the Portuguese escudo and the Spanish peseta were devalued. But the crisis reached its full climax in July 1993, following persistent speculative attacks against the French franc. On 30 July, the French and Belgian francs, the Danish kroner, the peseta and the escudo all fell close to their floor values. After a prolonged and acrimonious crisis meeting over the weekend, radical changes to the system were agreed. The bands allowing currencies to fluctuate by plus or minus 2.25 per cent were widened to 15 per cent. (The Netherlands chose to stick with the narrow bands.)

At the time this was seen as a major setback for the ERM and for the plans for EMU. In the event it had little impact on the move to a single currency.

---

policy-makers were sceptical that EMU would ever come about. Most were opposed to it on economic or political grounds, or both. Opposition in the UK was more widespread than in almost any other member state.

In 1988, the heads of government (Thatcher reluctantly) agreed to establish a committee to examine the prospects for EMU. It was chaired by the then President of the European Commission, Jacques Delors. The committee's report, signed by all members of the Committee, including the British representative, the Governor of the Bank

---

Box 4.4   The five economic tests

In October 1997, Chancellor Gordon Brown outlined five economic tests which would be used to determine whether there was a 'clear and unambiguous' case for British membership of the European single currency.

These tests were:

1   a sufficient degree of sustainable convergence between the UK and the economies of the single currency;
2   sufficient flexibility to enable the British economy to cope with the change;
3   whether joining EMU would create better conditions for businesses to undertake investment in Britain;
4   whether the British financial services industry would gain more from being within the single currency than outside;
5   whether membership of the single currency would be good for employment.

Although the government argued that these tests were intended to produce an objective assessment, many commentators believed that when the time came for a decision to be made, the criteria were sufficiently vague to enable a case to be made either way, depending on the government's political preferences.

---

of England, set out how EMU might be achieved by treating membership of the ERM as stage 1 and ending with monetary union. A modified version of this approach was adopted as the final plan for EMU (see Box 4.2). When the process was agreed at the Maastricht Summit of 1991, the UK and Denmark both secured opt-out arrangements to avoid their being obliged to join EMU. This did not deter the other EU members from pressing ahead and nor did the ERM crises of 1992 and 1993, when several ERM currencies came under sustained pressure (see Box 4.3).

By the mid-1990s it had become clear that EMU would not go ahead on the first possible date, 1 January 1997 (see Box 4.2). The terms of the Maastricht deal meant that it would therefore start on 1 January 1999. The Conservative government's position was that the UK would abstain from the first wave of members and would wait to see whether EMU worked before deciding to join. An almost identical position was adopted by the subsequent Labour government of Tony

Blair, although there was a much stronger presumption in favour of eventual membership (see Box 4.4). Out of office, and with a new leader, the official Conservative line hardened: membership was ruled out until at least 2007, with a strong presumption that the Conservatives would never favour membership of EMU.

Working with EMU

It was clear, though, that EMU would have a significant impact on British economic life and policy-making whether or not the UK joined. The new currency, the euro, came into being on 1 January 1999; it is scheduled to replace national currency notes and coins in EMU member states from January 2002. The euro's creation led to much speculation about its role as an international currency, especially in relation to the US dollar, the world's most important reserve currency. There were fears that London's position of pre-eminence as a financial centre – the largest foreign exchange market in the world and the largest financial market in Europe – would be damaged. Many large British companies were concerned about the potentially negative effects on their business which exclusion from the euro would bring. Their competitors within the euro zone benefited from the removal of exchange rate fluctuations, which British companies could not enjoy. These concerns were reflected in a number of associations set up in the late 1990s to campaign for early British entry to the single currency, though at least as many were established with the opposite purpose.

Some of the concerns expressed by opponents of the euro were legitimate economic ones. The most important of these was that the process of adjustment for some of the euro countries, newly subjected to a single monetary and exchange rate policy which could not take account of all their economic needs (known as the 'one size fits all' policy), would be painful, resulting in, for example, high unemployment or higher inflationary pressures. Some economists thought membership would make the UK particularly vulnerable because its economic cycle was out of step with the rest of Europe and because of the unusually close link between the housing market and short-term interest rates. At the same time, it was argued that the benefits of intra-European exchange rate stability and closer economic integration would be significant. Many economists felt that the economic arguments were finely balanced, but with some substantial downside risks – of being excluded at least temporarily from a successful venture, or being involved in a disastrous failure. Hence the British policy was to wait to see whether EMU worked before contemplating membership. Politically, the arguments raged on an altogether different plane, increasingly focusing on the threats posed by further erosion of national sovereignty.

The impact of EMU

There were two specific ways in which EMU affected British policy. The first related to the Maastricht conditions, which set out eligibility for countries that wanted to join the euro (see Box 4.5). After the experience of 1992, no British policy-maker was willing to contemplate sterling's re-entry into the ERM. But once the Maastricht

---

Box 4.5 The Maastricht criteria

In drawing up plans for EMU, it was recognised that economic convergence would be an important factor: that the participating countries should show signs that their inflation rates were converging and that their fiscal policies had broadly similar objectives. This would prevent too much strain being placed either on member states or on EMU itself. Member states therefore had to meet qualifying conditions for entry, known as the Maastricht criteria:

1   ERM: qualifying countries should be within the narrow bands without tension or depreciation for at least two years.
2   Inflation: the inflation rate should not exceed that of the best-performing member states by more than 1.5 percentage points.
3   Interest rates: average long-term interest rates should not exceed those of the best-performing member states by more than 2 percentage points.
4   Fiscal performance: total public debt should not exceed 60 per cent of GDP (unless it can be shown that the ratio is falling fast or approaching the target rate); and annual budget deficits should be no more that 3 per cent of GDP except in temporary or exceptional circumstances.

To ensure fiscal policy remained tightly controlled once a country had joined EMU, the Stability Pact was subsequently agreed on. This binds member states to the Maastricht fiscal criteria and threatens penalties on those which fail to meet them.

Treaty was signed, the UK set out to meet all the other entry criteria as a demonstration of its economic suitability: the Major government argued that the criteria for public debt, inflation and so on were policy objectives which any prudent government would seek to achieve. The length of the 1990–2 recession meant taking difficult decisions on spending and taxation in order to meet the target of lower borrowing. After the Labour Chancellor, Gordon Brown, took office in 1997, he ostentatiously stuck close to the Maastricht criteria when drawing up his own plans for spending and borrowing, going further indeed than was necessary simply to meet the criteria. He also introduced a significant degree of independence for the Bank of England – which was a further requirement for those countries gearing up to join EMU, as Brown pointed out (for further discussion of the Bank's independence, see Chapter 5). When eligibility for EMU membership was discussed by the EU in 1998, it was clear that the UK would have met all the entry conditions (except that of ERM membership).

The other direct effect on British policy came with the establishment in 1998 of a new EU ministerial and official committee to oversee the running of EMU. This committee, known first as Euro-X, and then Euro-11, replaced one of the key official committees of the EU, the Monetary Committee, which had, among other things, been responsible for the operation of the ERM. (The extent of political control over EMU which the new committee implied did not sit comfortably with the supposedly independent running of the single currency by the European Central Bank.) The UK tried hard to argue that it, too, should be a member of this new and key committee. This was firmly resisted by the eleven prospective members, culminating in a somewhat humiliating public row. Since negotiations over the committee took place during the British Presidency of the EU, the row was particularly unfortunate. Shortly afterwards, Prime Minister Blair found himself presiding over the initial meeting of heads of government which decided which countries could and would join EMU: a list which did not, of course, include the UK.

The UK's European future

The start of EMU marked an important stage in the development of the EU, and in the UK's role within it. Joining EMU would be seen as an important demonstration of British commitment to the EU. An endlessly postponed decision, or firmly ruling out membership, would strengthen the suspicions of those member states which see the UK as less than fully committed. This could undermine British influence still further when issues of considerable importance are being debated. Enlargement of the EU to include some of the former communist countries of Central Europe, and the terms of their membership, are issues which will directly affect the British economy, for instance.

At the same time, British policy-makers have to take account of the possibility that EMU could fail: that the economic strains imposed on those member states trying to integrate more closely with each other could become overwhelming. This is still a possibility if, for example, unemployment were to rise very sharply in some member states and not others. The challenge for policy-makers is to assess the balance of risks – and then make a decision, knowing that the price of making the wrong decision could be very high.

5   Inflation

Thirty years ago, in Britain at least, few non-economists would have been able to define inflation. Today, it would be at least as difficult to find anyone who did not know that it had something to do with rising prices. So deeply has inflation become embedded in the British psyche that even now, with inflation back down to levels not seen since the early 1960s, there are still complaints about the 'cost of living' going up. By contrast, few Britons could easily define *deflation* (falling prices).

These, of course, are impressionistic, anecdotal statements, not statistically based analyses. But inflation, like many areas of economic policy, is essentially impressionistic: it is not something policy-makers can tackle with facts alone. Perception is important in the framing of policy; expectations about future inflation are a critical factor in determining the outcome.

Defining the problem

The first thing to try to establish is why inflation is a problem and why it has come to be seen by many people as the economic scourge of the late twentieth century. It is not new, after all. Inflation has been a factor in economic performance at least as far back as Roman times. During the course of the third century AD, prices in the Roman Empire rose fifty-fold; China experienced inflation of around 6 per cent a year between 1190 and 1240; and Britain experienced more than one period of inflation during the sixteenth and seventeenth centuries, for example. Some countries have experienced bouts of *hyperinflation* (see Box 5.1). But before the middle of the twentieth century, periods of deflation were also common. In the UK, for example, prices in 1931 were *lower* than those in 1795. What made the second half of the

---

Box 5.1 Hyperinflation

At times in the 1970s, there were fears – misplaced – that the UK was in danger of experiencing hyperinflation: a period of very high and rapidly accelerating inflation. In fact, the UK has never experienced hyperinflation, although many other countries have. For example:

- during the American War of Independence, prices in Philadelphia rose by 1,000 per cent between 1779 and 1780;
- in Revolutionary France, prices rose by more than 38,000 per cent in six years;
- in Germany in 1922–3, the average monthly rise in prices was 322 per cent ;
- in Hungary in 1945–6, the average monthly rise in prices was 19,800 per cent.

More recently there have been periods of hyperinflation in Latin America, Ghana, Israel, Indonesia, Turkey, Russia and former states of the Soviet Union.

Typically, hyperinflation is accompanied by very rapid expansion of the money supply and by war or dramatic political change.

---

twentieth century distinctive was the prolonged and sustained nature of the inflationary experience in many countries – not least in the UK.

Put simply, inflation is a measure of the rate of increase in prices for the same goods: it therefore represents a fall in value of the unit of currency. This creates both economic and political problems. Stability is at the heart of the threat posed by inflation. In economic terms, it arbitrarily changes the relationship between various actors in the economy. As inflation rises, the value of capital falls. People's savings lose their value in terms of what they will buy. Those who rely on earned income do relatively better than those, such as pensioners, who rely on fixed incomes or savings, as workers are in a better position to ensure that their earnings rise in line with, or faster than, prices. Businesses face extra costs in periods of high inflation, apart from anything else because of the need for them to keep their prices (and cash flow) constantly under review. Economic uncertainty increases sharply because no one can predict what the rate of inflation will be. But because rising inflation creates expectations of further rises, people adjust their behaviour to take account of this. Workers lodge pay claims not just aimed at catching up with price rises to date, but which try to anticipate future inflation. Rising wage costs lead to higher prices, and the upward spiral of inflation is given a further twist. It is a classic example of the problems created by markets operating with imperfect information. And with economic uncertainty comes political uncertainty and the risk of political instability, as individuals within the economy seek to protect themselves as best they can.

Do governments mind?

Even at relatively low levels, then, inflation causes problems because of the uncertainty it generates and the arbitrary nature of its impact. Yet governments have in the past shown themselves to be remarkably tolerant of inflation. This is because governments are important beneficiaries of the phenomenon. Inflation can be a useful way for governments to raise extra revenue without drawing it to the attention of their citizens. They do this via *seigniorage* – the income which governments derive from issuing currency – and from the operation of fiscal drag: wages go up to keep pace with inflation but if the tax thresholds set by the government do not keep pace, people will end up paying more tax. Moreover, the cost of the government's debt falls, since *real* interest rates (the nominal level minus the rate of inflation) have in the past often been negative.

At the economic level, opinion is divided. Some economists have argued that inflation ceases to matter in a fully indexed economy, when everything rises in line with the change in prices. Indexation can certainly work to offset many of the more painful effects of inflation. At low rates of inflation it is also true that there may be little pressure on governments to act to curb it. Many voters care more about un-employment, for example, especially if they are themselves cushioned against the impact of inflation.

All this goes some way to explaining why British governments were relatively slow to act when inflation started to become a problem in the late 1960s and early 1970s. At the time, the UK's external position – its chronic balance-of-payments problems, coupled with fears about its inability to keep pace with its economic neighbours in terms of productivity and GDP per capita growth – seemed more pressing. Some politicians and economists voiced their fears. But the rhetoric was not matched by firm action. As long as inflation stayed at

Table 5.1   Inflation in the UK, 1950–89 (annual average rate)

Year	Rate	Year	Rate
1950	3.1	1970	6.4
1951	9.1	1971	9.4
1952	9.2	1972	7.6
1953	3.1	1973	9.2
1954	1.9	1974	16.1
1955	4.5	1975	24.2
1956	5.0	1976	16.5
1957	3.7	1977	15.8
1958	3.0	1978	8.3
1959	0.6	1979	13.4
1960	1.0	1980	18.0
1961	3.5	1981	11.9
1962	4.2	1982	8.6
1963	2.0	1983	4.6
1964	3.3	1984	5.0
1965	4.8	1985	6.1
1966	3.9	1986	3.4
1967	2.5	1987	4.2
1968	4.7	1988	4.9
1969	5.4	1989	7.8

See Table 5.2 for comparative inflation in the 1990s.
Data from the *Employment Gazette* (Department for Education and Employment, various issues).

3 per cent or 4 per cent a year, there seemed no need to worry unduly (see Table 5.1). Low unemployment seemed a more important goal.

Inflation can soon get out of hand

But, as became clear, there is no such thing as a stable rate of inflation. It has a built-in tendency to go on accelerating; it develops a momentum of its own. By the mid-1970s, with the annual inflation rate soaring to more than 25 per cent, there was talk of the dangers of hyperinflation. People and politicians became alarmed. By the late 1970s the inflation rate had fallen from its peak, though it was still uncomfortably high, and rising again. The experience had changed political and popular attitudes to inflation. When Margaret Thatcher won the 1979 election, her opposition to inflation and her commitment to bring it properly under control were crucial factors in her victory. Moreover, the new Prime Minister and her advisers had very clear views about how this was to be done. That these views turned out to be mistaken or difficult to implement was irrelevant to Thatcher's electoral success. The experience of the 1970s had helped sway public opinion, as had the fact that unemployment had soared at the same time, apparently giving the lie to the widely held belief that the one was a trade-off against the other (see Box 1.3, page 15).

It seems clear from the German experience of inflation in the twentieth century that popular support for counter-inflationary policies is a critical factor in the success of those policies. Germany had managed more successfully than most other countries to respond firmly and effectively to inflationary pressures resulting from the 1970s oil shocks. Inflation had risen by less, and for a shorter period, than elsewhere. But in 1922, and again after the Second World War, Germany had experienced hyperinflation (see Box 5.1 on page 99) and the folk memory of these had ensured lasting electoral support for counter-inflationary policy. Thatcher hoped for the same support as a result of the UK's more recent experience. As it turned out, these hopes were premature because of mistakes made by her own government.

Helped by the new government's generous pay deals for public sector workers, inflation continued to climb sharply after the 1979 election – it went up to 19.8 per cent in 1980. From then on, it began to decline quite sharply, although there is much argument about why it did so (see below). But in the late 1980s, inflation started to rise again. Having successfully begun to influence people's expectations about future inflation and thus their behaviour, the government displayed ineptitude by making the same mistake as some of its predecessors: it showed a willingness to tolerate relatively low inflation. The Chancellor, Nigel Lawson, appeared more intent on promoting British growth, cutting taxes and seeking to find ways of joining the ERM than on ensuring that inflation was on a downward path. By the time inflation had touched 5 per cent it had developed its own momentum. A famously described 'temporary blip' suddenly turned into a steeply accelerating rise. Inflation was up to 10.9 per cent at its peak in September and October 1990.

Ironically, it was this second episode of high inflation which seems to have been a watershed. For the past decade all political parties have placed low inflation at the very top of their economic priorities: it has become the *sine qua non* of government economic policies. All other policy objectives are defined in this context: attainable only within a framework of low inflation.

Controlling inflation

As Thatcher came to realise, the big challenge facing policy-makers is how to get inflation down and then keep it low. In the 1960s and 1970s, most popular analyses of inflation cited two principal causes: demand pull and cost push. In other words, inflationary pressures could be generated when demand in the economy outstripped supply (a familiar problem in post-war Britain); or these pressures could arise from a sharp rise in the cost base – the oil price shock is perhaps the best example.

Policies were developed to deal with both forms of pressure; these became known as prices and incomes policies. The Wilson government set up the Prices and Incomes Board in 1965, the first of many attempts to regulate the economy in this way. The Heath government established the Price Commission in 1973 with substantive powers to prevent or delay price rises. A statutory incomes policy was also introduced under the Heath government, imposing limits on the rise in wages which employers could offer. The Labour government which took over in 1974 added price subsidies – paid for by government taxation and borrowing – to its armoury. None of these policies seemed to be capable of bringing about more than a temporary respite from inflationary pressures. They were unpopular both with business, which objected to price controls, and with unions, then far more powerful, which resented the obstacles being put in the way of their achieving better deals for their members.

In a sense, these policies failed because they largely tackled the symptoms of inflation and not its causes. Workers objected, understandably, to having limits imposed on pay increases which were below the rate at which they could see prices were rising. These limits cut into their purchasing power: they were, in effect, being asked to accept a fall in their standard of living. It did not matter that living standards had risen steadily since 1945, or that pay rises were often not matched by corresponding increases in productivity. Incomes policies were an attempt to depress demand, either voluntarily or compulsorily.

But they did not, ultimately, change attitudes to or expectations about inflation.

An alternative approach

Milton Friedman (see Box 1.2 on page 14) and other economists argued that the failure of these policies was inevitable, because they did not recognise that inflation was a monetary phenomenon. By this they meant that inflation was the result of too rapid an expansion of the supply of money in an economy – in part, at least, the result of governments' willingness to print money to finance their borrowing. This, according to Friedman *et al.*, was what happened in the late 1960s in the US when President Johnson chose to finance the expensive and unpopular war in Vietnam without raising taxes.

The monetarists' analysis certainly sounded plausible: in essence they were offering a rational explanation for what is self-evidently the root cause of inflation – too much money chasing too few goods. For politicians desperate to find an effective solution to the problems of inflation, the monetarist prescription was tantalisingly simple: control the supply of money circulating within the economy. Ration money just like any other good, by price – the interest rate. When inflation was rising, it meant that the money supply was growing too fast; higher interest rates would curb this growth, and would in due course halt and then reverse the rise in inflation.

When she became leader of the Conservative Party in 1975, Margaret Thatcher sought the advice of the monetarist school. By 1979, when she became Prime Minister, she and her government were ready to act. As we saw in Chapter 2, the Labour Chancellor Denis Healey (in office from 1974 to 1979) was the first to introduce monetary targeting in 1976, under pressure from the IMF (and he was more successful at meeting these targets than any of his successors). But for the Thatcher government control of inflation using tight management of the money supply was the centrepiece of its strategy.

Easier in theory than practice

Unfortunately, monetarism proved harder to implement in practice than some of the theorists had suggested. The achievements of the

Thatcher government in reducing inflation over its first seven years came in spite of a striking failure to control the money supply. Before examining why inflation came down in this period, it is important first to understand why monetary control failed. As with many areas of

---

Box 5.2   The Medium-Term Financial Strategy

The MTFS was first published alongside the 1980 budget. It was largely the brainchild of Nigel Lawson, later to be Chancellor of the Exchequer (1983–9) but at the time Financial Secretary, a junior ministerial post in the Treasury. Lawson started from the assumption that it made sense for the government to set out its medium-term aims. Critics, including some other ministers as well as civil servants, thought this was a mistake: it offered hostages to fortune if the forecasts were not delivered. But for Lawson and his supporters this was precisely the point – the MTFS was intended to be a self-imposed constraint on government policy.

The MTFS said the aim of the government was to bring down inflation and create the conditions for the sustained growth of output and employment by gradually reducing the growth of the stock (or supply) of money. Target ranges for this growth were explicitly set out. The MTFS also laid out the government's plans to reduce government borrowing as a percentage of GDP. This partly reflected the belief at the time that high public borrowing would mean higher interest rates – something Lawson subsequently came to regard more sceptically.

The MTFS failed spectacularly to meet its monetary targets:

Year	Target range for sterling M3 (%)[a]	Actual outturn
1980–1	7–11	18.4
1981–2	6–10	12.8
1982–3	5–9	11.1
1983–4	4–8	9.5

[a]Percentage range of growth in sterling M3 permitted.
Data from HM Treasury.

The MTFS served only to highlight the difficulties of monetary control as a means of reducing inflation. Eventually, the MTFS was abandoned as a separate policy tool. But it is worth remembering that governments have continued the habit of setting out their medium-term objectives, although they now make them in a rather more low-key way.

economics, there are considerable gaps in our knowledge of how the macroeconomy works. This inevitably provides scope for disagreement among professional economists and policy-makers, and the arguments about monetarism are no exception. These arguments – which still rumble on – centred on which measure of the money supply to use, and on the relative importance of the velocity of money – the speed with which it circulates around the economy. But the attempts to exert control over the British money supply in the early 1980s also illustrate another powerful truth about economic policy-making, touched on in Chapter 3: experiments in the real world cannot be conducted in isolation from other developments which may themselves have an impact on the policy under scrutiny.

The government announced its plans for controlling the money supply in the 1979 budget; these were considerably refined in 1980 when it published its Medium-Term Financial Strategy (MTFS) (see Box 5.2). The MTFS was designed to influence people's expectations about future economic policy and thus their behaviour. The government began by targeting sterling M3, a specific measure of the money supply. This decision was not endorsed by the monetarists, although the critics were not united in their favoured alternative. Indeed, the monetarists continued – and still continue – to argue among themselves, sometimes bitterly, about issues such as the appropriate measure to target.

Sterling M3 was what is known as a broad measure of the money supply. It included cash – the total amount of notes and coin in circulation in the economy – plus many short-term bank deposits. Alternative targets included the narrowest measure of money – just cash – and much wider measures, which included longer-term bank and building society deposits. These arguments were complicated by disagreement about the *predictive* value of a particular indicator. If you want to know when to take action to curb inflationary pressures, it is no use relying on what is known as a *coincident* indicator – for example, a measure of money which rises *with* inflation rather than *ahead* of it. You want an indicator which will warn you of an impending rise in inflation and enable you to take the appropriate action to prevent it.

These arguments began to seem even more arcane when sterling M3 promptly soared – exceeding its targets and appearing not to respond to the substantial rise in interest rates implemented by the government. Other monetary targets behaved no more reliably. Charles Goodhart, then an adviser at the Bank of England, currently an academic and a member of the Bank's MPC, even propounded a new law, Goodhart's Law, which noted that monetary indicators started to behave erratically once targeted by government.

Inflation nonetheless fell sharply from 1981. Several factors seem to explain this. The most obvious was the impact of the government's high interest rate policy. The economy moved into an unusually deep recession in 1980–1 (the deepest since the war) which had the effect, among other things, of reducing demand very sharply. This was, said monetarist critics, simply the old-fashioned way of squeezing inflation out of the economy.

Then there was the impact of the relaxation of the 'corset'. This was the name given to a system of supplementary special deposits introduced in 1978 as a form of control on bank lending: banks which lent too much were penalised by having to deposit funds with the Bank of England on which they earned no interest. The Thatcher government decided to abolish these in 1980 because the banks had found it too easy to get around the corset, using other means to lend money. It was recognised that removing the corset would have a temporary effect on sterling M3, as banks reverted to lending in the normal way. What no one had foreseen was the scale of this effect: the sterling M3 measure of the money supply rose by 5 per cent in one month between June and July 1980 – causing great alarm in the financial markets and undermining confidence in the government's attempts at monetary control.

Other changes were being introduced as well, in line with the government's belief in deregulating financial markets. Exchange controls were abolished. The government started to deregulate building societies. These institutions had traditionally been very staid: they lent money almost exclusively to finance house purchase, and depositors usually left funds in their accounts for long periods. Now they became free to offer a wide range of banking services, including current accounts. Yet building society deposits had been treated quite differently from bank deposits in the various measures of money supply. These changes added confusion to the picture of what was happening.

In spite of the difficulties of demonstrating the link between monetary control and inflation in practice, the existence of the link itself became much more widely accepted during the 1980s. Placing undue emphasis on a specific – and ultimately unattainable – monetary target was criticised, the search for a monetary solution to the problem of inflation less so.

The elusive solution

But those trying to construct an effective and acceptable counter-inflationary policy needed more than a shift in the conventional wisdom. The politicians – the Prime Minister and Chancellor – still hankered after a simple solution: a clear anti-inflationary anchor, which by the mid-1980s Nigel Lawson (Chancellor from 1983 to 1989) thought he had found in the ERM (see Box 2.5 on page 48). The German mark was the dominant currency in the ERM, and since the late 1940s Germany had established an enviable reputation for low inflation. Lawson concluded that linking sterling to the German mark would bring the benefits of association with a low-inflation economy: the financial markets would quickly recognise that the government was similarly committed to keeping inflation down.

As we noted in Chapter 3, however, the Chancellor is not the sole guardian of economic policy. He must convince the Prime Minister, above all, of the wisdom of the course he advocates. For a number of reasons, not the least of which was Margaret Thatcher's instinctive mistrust both of Europe in general and the ERM in particular, she opposed British membership. Unlike Lawson, she did not want British monetary policy made subservient to policies operated elsewhere.

More than a decade after this crucial policy disagreement, the two opposing camps dispute each other's analysis of the rise in inflation from 1987 onwards, a rise which took most officials and ministers by surprise. Those who favoured an exchange rate anchor claim that failing to join the ERM meant a missed opportunity to tackle inflation once and for all. Lawson's critics believe he was distracted by his efforts to bring about a policy reversal and failed to recognise the inflationary pressures building up in the economy once more. His decision secretly to shadow the mark (see Chapter 2, page 47) led him to cut interest rates to keep the pound stable; this added to the inflationary pressures building up in the economy. By the time the government recognised the need to raise interest rates sharply, the damage had been done.

A turning point in attitudes

The inflationary surge of the late 1980s was a turning point in terms of counter-inflationary policy in the UK. Thatcher and the man who succeeded her in 1990, John Major, displayed even greater determination than previously not just to bring inflation down – this had, after all, been achieved once – but to eradicate it as a serious economic threat. At the same time, the impact of the Thatcher government's failure to keep inflation at bay had powerful implications both for the opposition Labour Party and for the electorate as a whole. Labour now saw inflation as a stick with which to beat the government. In doing so, however, the opposition party was obliged to take an equally firm stand against inflation and to commit itself – publicly and repeatedly – to keep inflation low, to aim to be more successful than the Conservatives in pursuing low or zero inflation as a long-term goal. The Labour Party had three leaders between 1992 and 1994, and it radically revised its political platform. But the commitment to low inflation remained unaltered: it became the centrepiece of Labour's economic policy. Moreover, low inflation appears to have substantial popular support as a goal.

Consensus on the goal

The policy arguments about inflation, then, have come to be arguments about the *means* of achieving the goal, not about the goal itself. No mainstream policy-maker now argues that there may be a trade-off between inflation and other economic objectives in the long term. There is now also less disagreement about the means used to control inflation, although this is in part a result of greater success in controlling it, and in part because the policy adopted by successive governments since 1992 has been far more eclectic and less dogmatic.

For policy-makers, recent success has come at a high price. The argument over ERM membership which ended when the UK joined in October 1990 had been largely conducted at the political level, among ministers. (It had, for example, been the subject of argument among officials in the early 1980s, when the Foreign and Commonwealth Office (FCO) sought to persuade a then sceptical Treasury and Bank of England about the benefits of membership. By the mid-1980s most Treasury officials had come round to favouring membership.) But far from resolving the issue, British membership of the ERM compounded the economic difficulties which policy-makers, at official and ministerial level, encountered over the following two years.

The ERM crisis

Again, the arguments are complex because of the fundamental difficulty in policy-making: having to implement policy in the real world, far removed from laboratory conditions. Three factors appeared to work against the sustainability of sterling's position within the ERM; it is not possible to be certain whether any one of these alone would have made the pound's position unworkable. Sterling joined the ERM when British inflation was significantly higher than in the other member states: membership was justified on the grounds of *prospective* falls in inflation. Economic theory would usually suggest that the exchange rate would need to adjust downwards to take account of the inflation differential, something ERM membership made very difficult. The UK was also on the brink of a prolonged recession, largely the result of substantial rises in interest rates between 1988 and 1990 (the cut in rates which coincided with ERM entry still left them at 14 per cent). This meant that the UK was cyclically soon out of step with other EU countries, which did not move into recession until 1992–3, and that the British economy was less well equipped to cope with rising European interest rates, which had not been anticipated in 1990. These high interest rates were themselves a result of the third factor, which has most often been cited as the underlying reason for the ERM policy failure: German reunification in 1990. Reunification created an asymmetric shock to the ERM itself: that is, it was an external shock affecting one member – Germany – but not the others. Reunification imposed huge costs on the German government budget; these created significant inflationary pressures on the newly reunited economy, partly because of the government's reluctance to raise taxes. The Bundesbank sought to quash these pressures through a policy of high interest rates. Had Germany not been the anchor of the ERM, the impact might not have been so great; but because of the mark's central role, other countries were obliged to raise their interest rates as well, in order to keep within their currency bands. The British government avoided the rate rises of December 1991, fearful of making the recession worse and more prolonged: and managed to get away with this tactic for several months.

The real trouble began in June 1992, when the financial markets were thrown into turmoil after the Danish electorate voted against the Treaty of Maastricht, a vote with enormous implications because the Treaty enshrined Europe's plans for EMU. Several ERM currencies, but particularly the pound and the Italian lira, came under substantial pressure. The British government remained reluctant to risk prolonging or worsening the recession still further by raising interest rates to defend sterling. The crisis for sterling worsened through the summer and on 16 September, after a day of unprecedented market pressure, British membership of the ERM was suspended indefinitely. We have already noted the political ramifications of these events in Chapter 2, and the implications for exchange rate policy will be discussed in Chapter 8. But the consequences for counter-inflationary policy were equally far-reaching.

It is important to note what happened to British inflation during ERM membership. Already past its peak in 1990 as a result of the high interest rate strategy introduced in 1988, inflation continued to fall sharply. Policy-makers felt sufficiently confident of the downward momentum to cut interest rates several times during this period. They argued publicly that this was possible because of ERM membership; that the ERM policy itself was a clear indication of the government's overriding commitment to low inflation. But the sharp falls in inflation, coupled with a more prolonged recession than anticipated, created increasing dissatisfaction with the level of interest rates. These, critics argued, were higher than necessary to combat inflation; the implicit point was that protecting the exchange rate and the UK's position in the ERM now had higher priority than fighting inflation.

It is not possible even now to distinguish between cause and effect with any degree of certainty. Did inflation fall in the UK because of ERM membership, or in spite of it? Would it have been more difficult to achieve falling inflation without the ERM? Even those not essentially supportive of the decision to join the ERM have acknowledged that the period of ERM membership enabled the government to cut interest rates more rapidly than would otherwise have been the case, consistent with efforts to bear down on inflation.

Targeting inflation

September 1992 marked the end, in the UK at least, of attempts to target intermediate objectives in counter-inflationary policy. Unexpectedly bereft of the central plank of economic policy, officials and ministers hurriedly put together a replacement. The experience with monetary targeting and the exchange rate had made it clear that policy could not be based on one indicator alone, which might prove un-reliable or unsustainable. Instead, the new policy talked about the need to take account of a range of economic indicators. These included growth, consumer demand, earnings levels and unemployment rates, as well as the money supply and the exchange rate.

But the most distinctive feature of the new policy was the decision to target inflation directly. The government would in future announce a specific objective for inflation, explicitly aiming to achieve that level about two years further on, to take account of the time lags involved in any counter-inflationary strategy. Although the government continued to keep a close watch on the retail price index, the most commonly known measure of inflation, it chose to target what is known as the underlying rate of inflation: this excludes the cost of mortgage interest payments, which are generally regarded as distorting the picture of what is happening to inflation (since they are themselves affected by changes in interest rates). Initially, the government said it would aim for a range of 1–4 per cent, with a future objective being to bring inflation to 2.5 per cent or below by 1997 (the end of the Parliament). The target was to be reviewed each year.

The success of the new policy was remarkable, not least because few predicted it. The size of the devaluation which took place in the months after the pound floated in late 1992 was something of the order of 20 per cent (slightly more at some points). Traditional macroeconomic theory suggested a significant rise in inflation, after an appropriate interval, in such circumstances. This did not happen; inflation instead continued to fall, surprising most commentators. By the time of the 1997 election, inflation was only slightly outside the target range.

Because of its success, the policy has also survived for longer than any other in recent British experience. Norman Lamont's successor as Chancellor in 1993, Kenneth Clarke, introduced some refinements, but did nothing substantively to alter the policy. Much more significant was the Labour government's decision to stick with the broad policy approach, albeit with significant modifications, when it assumed power in 1997.

A record of success

Since 1992, the UK's inflation performance has been better than at any time since the 1960s. This is partly a result of the decision to pursue a more eclectic approach in judging inflationary pressures. Gone is the attempt at *automaticity* – the belief in a clear and identifiable link with the money supply or the exchange rate or, indeed, retail price movements or wages. Instead, all of those factors are taken into account, as well as many others, as the policy-makers try to arrive at a balanced judgement of the inflationary pressures in the economy and likely to affect the outturn for inflation at some point in the future.

Interest rates, however, remain central to counter-inflationary strategy. They are the central policy variable, to be adjusted to take account of changing economic conditions. And it is the way in which interest rates are adjusted which has seen some of the more far-reaching policy changes since 1992. After the turmoil of the 1980s and the spectacular collapse of its economic strategy in 1992, the Major government decided that openness and transparency had to be an important element in creating a new policy framework. Meetings between the Chancellor and the Governor of the Bank of England, to review monetary policy, were made more regular, taking place at pre-arranged monthly intervals.

Clarke made further changes in 1993. Once any adjustment in interest rates had been agreed, the Governor was given discretion over the timing of the change. The minutes of the monthly meeting between the two men and their officials were published after a six-week delay (exactly mirroring long-established practice at the US Federal Reserve Board). The decision to publish was, in theory, designed to reduce the impact of the electoral cycle, by making explicit any disagreement between the Chancellor – who might have political motives, for instance, in wanting to reduce or raise interest rates – and the Governor, supposed to be above such considerations.

Independence for the Bank of England

When Labour's Gordon Brown became Chancellor in May 1997, he took everyone by surprise (not least the Governor of the Bank of England) by going much further down the route of de-politicising monetary policy. Within a few days of taking office, he gave full responsibility for all interest rate decisions to the Bank of England. The Chancellor would continue to set the inflation target, published annually in the form of an open letter to the Governor. But it would be up to the Bank to ensure the target was met. Failure would require the

Governor to write a formal public letter of explanation to the Chancellor. The Bank had long been campaigning – discreetly – for independence and two former Conservative Chancellors, Nigel Lawson and Norman Lamont, had come out publicly in support of the idea after leaving office. Independence brought the Bank of England into line with the Bundesbank, the US Federal Reserve and a growing number of central banks around the world. An independent central bank is also one of the conditions for joining EMU in Europe (see Chapter 4).

A new policy framework for the independent Bank was established by Chancellor Brown. The MPC was set up, all nine members of which are appointed by the Chancellor. It is chaired by the Governor; and both Deputy Governors (previously there was only one) also sit on the MPC. Other members come from both within the Bank and outside; some of the outsiders spend all their time at the Bank, while others are part-time. The MPC meets monthly, according to a pre-arranged time-table, usually in the first week of the month, with any decision on interest rates announced at the end of a series of meetings. Minutes of the MPC discussions – including details of how each member voted on interest rates – were initially published after a six-week delay; in 1998, this was reduced to two weeks.

Measuring the success of the new policy arrangements and the conduct of the MPC is difficult for a number of reasons. To make a detailed assessment would require a longer period of operation. This is partly because of the time lags associated with inflation. As already noted, policy actions do not usually have their full effect for about two years, so something like a five-year period would be needed to see whether the MPC had been able consistently to meet the inflation target over a period of three or four years.

It is also quite difficult even to define what would represent success for the MPC. On one level it might simply mean hitting the target. The policy-makers of the MPC, however, are unlikely to be completely immune from outside pressure and are certainly not immune from inaccurate assessment of economic developments. They are independent of the political process, or at least they are intended to be. In practice they are likely to find themselves under pressure if ministers – sometimes for reasons other than those directly connected with counter-inflationary policy – want to see interest rates go up – or, more likely, down. This occurred during the winter of 1998–9, when some commentators voiced disquiet at the apparent pressure being put on the MPC.

Ultimately, the MPC members – like all policy-makers – are being asked to make a judgement: one based on the information available about what is happening in the economy; forecasts about what will happen to it (often conflicting); their assessment of these figures; and their collective experience and wisdom. Chapter 3 analysed in some detail the problems these factors pose for policy-makers. Unusually for policy-makers who are not politicians, the members of the MPC are putting their own personal reputations at stake, and this will also be a factor, though one impossible to quantify, in their deliberations and decisions.

Inflation beaten?

There is another complicating factor, also touched on in Chapter 3, and which is particularly important in the context of counter-inflationary policy in the 1990s and beyond. Inflation, and the choice of policy response, has, as we have seen, long been a contentious issue. This proved no less true in the late 1990s as inflation in the UK fell to unexpectedly low levels. Two distinct views of the role of inflation in the British economy emerged after 1992. There are those who believe that inflation is no longer a threat and that it need no longer be a central issue of policy. Others take the opposite view, that inflation is a constant threat and that to believe otherwise is to be dangerously complacent. Policy-makers have to pick their way through this mine-field.

The divergence of views arose partly because of the unexpected path of inflation following sterling's departure from the ERM – it defied the conventional wisdom by continuing to fall, in spite of the devaluation which had taken place. But as is always the case when trying to determine cause and effect for economic policy purposes, other relevant developments were taking place in the global economy at the same time. Inflationary pressures worldwide weakened significantly during the 1990s. Commodity prices continued to fall. The oil price fell sharply – to a level which by early 1999 was close in real terms to that in 1972 (although it rose again towards the end of that year). These factors helped reduce inflationary pressures in the UK. But some economists now think that the 1970s and 1980s were the exception, and that inflation has therefore largely subsided as a threat. These commentators point to the threat of deflation in some countries,

Table 5.2 Comparative inflation in the 1990s (average annual rates)

	UK	US	France	Germany	Japan
1990	9.5	5.4	3.4	2.7	3.1
1991	5.9	4.2	3.2	3.7	3.3
1992	3.7	3.0	2.4	5.1	1.7
1993	1.6	3.0	4.4	2.1	1.2
1994	2.5	2.6	1.7	2.8	0.7
1995	3.4	2.8	1.8	1.7	-0.1
1996	2.5	2.9	2.0	1.4	0.1
1997	3.1	2.3	1.2	1.9	1.7
1998	3.4	1.6	0.6	0.9	0.6

Data from HM Treasury.

most notably Japan, to illustrate the view that the risk is of fighting the
wrong battle.

Other developments, however, may suggest the need for caution.
Even in the 1990s, British inflation remained higher than in many
other industrial countries. Earnings continued to rise significantly
faster than prices and than in other countries – as they did throughout
Britain's era of high inflation. Interest rates, though comparatively low
by British standards, remained much higher than elsewhere, implying
subdued but extant inflationary pressures (see Table 5.2). It is not
difficult to see why the MPC adopted a cautious approach to its task
and why British politicians, scarred by their experience of counter-
inflationary policies, continued to be obsessed by inflation.

For many years, constructing an effective policy to deal with inflation – and one which could command popular support – proved to
be almost insurmountable in Britain. Inflation can be difficult to assess
until it is too late to prevent it reaching undesirable levels. Because
of the random nature of its impact, some individuals and companies
will in any case always benefit from inflation; those who lose out may
be weaker, less vocal, or simply ignorant of the damage being inflicted
on them. The time lag between policy action and the result is substantial and can add to the pressure for equivocation, since policies to
combat inflation are invariably painful and therefore unpopular in the
short term.

The benefits of a successful policy, by contrast, are intangible. A
low-inflation economy is not something ordinary citizens easily relate

to: indeed, money illusion – that is, a preference for large nominal pay rises, which may nevertheless be negative after taking account of inflation – is extremely powerful. Few individuals or businesses readily accept that stable inflation – which they might find an acceptable alternative to further painfully achieved reductions – is simply not sustainable. In periods of low inflation policy-makers find themselves trying to defend a policy to deal with something most people do not recognise, or do not care about. It is not a rewarding task, yet history shows that inflation is a fearsome force for social destruction.

6　The labour market

Employment and unemployment have been matters of public concern since before the Industrial Revolution. Working conditions, child labour, skills shortages: these were all issues which preoccupied policy-makers in one way or another during the eighteenth and nineteenth centuries. But the idea that economic policy could play an active role in improving the functioning of the labour market is one particularly associated with the twentieth century.

As with so many areas of economic life in Britain, the Second World War played a pivotal role in changing attitudes. The wartime coalition government recognised that the high levels of unemployment seen in the 1930s were no longer acceptable: policy should be directed towards preventing its recurrence. For three decades after the war, it was largely successful. It gradually came to be realised, however, that while the post-war commitment to full employment might be socially desirable, it was increasingly difficult to achieve at an acceptable economic price. In the last twenty years or so there has been a transformation in the attitudes of British politicians and policy-makers towards the role of government in the labour market and towards the objectives of policy. Significantly, there is a remarkable degree of consensus about this role – possibly more than at any time since the early 1960s.

Full employment

As we saw in Chapters 1 and 2, the post-war commitment to full employment was underpinned by the 1942 Beveridge report and the 1944 White Paper *Employment Policy*. Policy was therefore directed first at providing a job for everyone (or at least every man) who wanted one; and second at providing adequate levels of welfare assistance to those who could not get a job or who were unable to work. For decades the consequence of these objectives was a commitment to the management of demand in the economy – the idea being that government could provide the necessary stimulus to create sufficient jobs – and a commitment to public spending sufficient both to achieve the demand stimulus and provide government help for those who could not find a job or who were unable to work. Gradually, however, these commitments overwhelmed successive governments. The inflationary consequences of the policies became impossible to ignore, as did the implications for public spending. Moreover, during the 1970s it became clear that the principal policy objective of full employment was not being met – at least not in ways which satisfied the expectations of either the public or policy-makers. Unemployment started to rise inexorably, no matter what governments did (see Table 6.1).

The jobless figures continued to rise even more sharply after 1979, but at that point the Thatcher government had explicitly abandoned the commitment to full employment. Margaret Thatcher did not advocate high unemployment; she merely argued that governments could not do very much about it directly in the short term, especially if they were trying to reduce inflation. Her victory in the 1983 general election, against a backdrop of still rising unemployment, showed that this was no longer a barrier to electoral success. Unemployment was falling by the time Thatcher won the 1987 election; but her successor as Conservative Prime Minister, John Major, won the 1992 election with unemployment rising once again. Governments no longer had to keep unemployment down at any price, giving policy-makers the chance to pursue alternative labour market strategies which might create the conditions for lower unemployment in the longer term. What these alternative strategies should be, however, was the subject of much argument. The debate intensified after the recession of the early 1990s, when unemployment in the UK fell sharply, much faster and further than the predictions of most forecasters and against the trend of many other industrial countries. It was clear that there was still much to learn about the causes of, and therefore the solutions to, high unemployment.

Problems of definition

Even defining full employment is difficult. The figure cannot be zero: there will always be people who are in the middle of changing jobs;

Table 6.1   The rise in unemployment

Year	% of workforce unemployed	Year	% of workforce unemployed
1945	0.5	1972	3.7
1946	1.9	1973	2.6
1947	1.4	1974	2.5
1948	1.3	1975	3.9
1949	1.2	1976	5.4
1950	1.6	1977	5.7
1951	1.3	1978	5.6
1952	2.2	1979	4.0
1953	1.8	1980	5.0
1954	1.5	1981	8.3
1955	1.2	1982	9.5
1956	1.3	1983	10.5
1957	1.6	1984	10.6
1958	2.2	1985	10.8
1959	2.3	1986	11.2
1960	1.7	1987	9.9
1961	1.6	1988	8.2
1962	2.1	1989	6.3
1963	2.6	1990	5.7
1964	1.7	1991	7.8
1965	1.5	1992	9.6
1966	1.5	1993	10.3
1967	2.4	1994	9.4
1968	2.4	1995	8.1
1969	2.3	1996	7.4
1970	2.5	1997	5.7
1971	3.4	1998	4.8

Because of numerous changes in the way unemployment statistics are measured, a consistent run of figures over a long period is impossible to obtain, but the following figures are very roughly comparable. The most important break comes in 1988. Before that the figures are those which appear in the *International Historical Statistics for Europe 1750–1988* (which are derived from a variety of sources); from 1988 they come from the *Economic Trends Annual Supplement*. The table nevertheless shows the significant rise in unemployment over the period.

others who work only seasonally; some who do not want to work at all; and still others who are incapable of working, because of disability or ill-health. The Beveridge report suggested that the lowest unemployment rate attainable was probably around 3 per cent. In fact, for twenty years after the war, unemployment was significantly lower than that; it tended to stay within the 1–2 per cent range, which came to be regarded as full employment. It was only as unemployment started to rise above this range in the late 1960s and 1970s that policy-makers began to doubt whether these low rates were sustainable.

Measuring employment and unemployment is actually quite difficult. Which is the better measure of economically active people: the percentage of the workforce which is *employed*, or the number of people or percentage of the workforce which is *unemployed*? How do we define the workforce: everyone who is *capable* of doing a job, or everyone who *wants* one? Should part-time work be included? Do we count all those able to work who are without a job, or just those actively seeking work, or just those claiming unemployment benefit?

These are only some of the enormously complex issues which policy-makers have struggled to grasp. They are not exercises in semantics, as any labour economist will confirm. The definition adopted can crucially affect the resulting figures, which in turn can affect both the policy adopted and people's expectations. In Britain, two principal measures were used until the 1990s: the claimant count, the government's own calculation based on the number of people claiming unemployment benefit; and the International Labour Organisation (ILO) survey figure, which used a broader definition. During the 1980s, the Thatcher government was heavily criticised because of the large number of changes made to its claimant count definition: critics argued that these were devious attempts to make the unemployment figure appear lower than it was (by, for example, excluding young unemployed people on training courses). The Labour government elected in 1997 decided to use as the official measure the ILO definition – which is standardised across countries, making international comparisons easier.

So what is full employment?

Refining the measures of unemployment unfortunately gets us no nearer to deciding what full employment is. After the surge in unemployment in the 1970s and 1980s, it became generally accepted that the assumptions of the early post-war period were wrong. Those low unemployment rates of 1 or 2 per cent were written off as an aberration. The actual rate of full employment was reckoned to be more like 7 or 8 per cent. These estimates then had to be scaled back as the jobless rate continued to fall in the 1990s. The rate which is now seen by much of the economics profession and by many policy-makers as crucial is the somewhat inelegantly named NAIRU: the non-accelerating inflation rate of unemployment. This is the lowest level of unemployment which does not increase inflationary pressures on the economy. But this has made the policy-makers' task no easier: most people (though not all) agree the NAIRU exists, but no one is able to demonstrate conclusively what it is.

The end of Keynesianism

The problems of definition have become less pressing, however, as the focus of policy has shifted. In the days when unemployment was thought of principally as a function of demand in the economy, governments were keen to stimulate demand when the jobless total showed signs of rising; this they did by a combination of tax cuts and spending increases. When unemployment fell – and when inflationary pressures started to build up – these measures were reversed ('applying the brakes', as politicians termed it). This whole approach was one where the government saw itself as having a central and crucial role in determining the overall level of demand in the economy which manifested itself in output and jobs.

Gradually, however, as we have seen in earlier chapters, this approach to the economy was undermined, in two ways. First, the cost of the policies became politically and economically unsustainable; and secondly, they no longer appeared to work. The one reinforced the other in the search for alternative approaches. Two major factors came to be seen as significant. One was the politically counter-productive impact of the second arm of the Beveridge commitment: generous welfare provision for the unemployed was thought to provide a substantial disincentive to seek work. The other was the structure of the labour market itself, which was increasingly seen as too rigid, making the creation of new jobs more difficult than it need be.

We will examine the public spending implications of the cost of labour market policies more closely in Chapter 9. But it is worth noting here the way in which these costs accumulated, which eventually forced policy-makers to reassess their approach. Unemployment benefit is notionally an entitlement paid to workers who find themselves without a job; it is an entitlement because of their compulsory National Insurance contributions (and those paid by their employers). This is notional in the sense that these contributions no longer fully fund such payments. The entitlement is now valid for six months (it used to be one year). But as the provisions of the welfare state became more generous, so did the extent of the benefits available to the unemployed. Although unemployment benefit itself is time-limited, income support is available to the long-term unemployed; this provides benefits according to need, depending on whether the claimant has children or other dependants, for example. Other, linked benefits are also available.

Disincentives to work

With provision on such a scale – generous by US standards, less so in comparison with other European countries – it is easy to see what the cost implications are. A benefit system largely constructed to cope with unemployment at less than one million is going to be enormously expensive when the figure rises to three million or more, as it did in the 1980s. Moreover, welfare programmes fall into the category of demand-determined spending: since they reflect automatic entitlement to certain categories of citizen, they cannot be controlled in the same way that the government can put a limit on, for instance, spending on the arts.

The cost of these programmes, therefore, provided a strong incentive to look at alternative ways of dealing with unemployment. Welfare benefits, after all, treat the symptoms, not the cause. They were originally intended to provide a temporary safety net for those unable to find work. But as the costs grew, so did the evidence mount of a growing number of people heavily and persistently dependent on benefits. Economists began to examine whether these benefits were themselves acting as a disincentive to the recipient's search for work.

They indisputably are, in some cases. The calculations involved are simple and do not imply any moral judgement. For an unemployed worker with dependants, the structure of the benefit system is such that it becomes difficult to see how he or she could be better off by taking work. The effective marginal rate of tax paid by those just moving from unemployment to work can be as high as 90 per cent: for every one pound earned, around ninety pence is lost in benefits to which he or she is no longer entitled. These factors also make it difficult for one partner in a two-adult household to take low-paid work if the other is unemployed. The rules of the benefit system mean that to do so is uneconomic because of the value of benefits lost.

Tackling the real problem

Policy-makers began to realise that a benefit system designed as a safety net had actually become a trap for a small but significant number of people. At the same time, convincing research showed that tackling unemployment effectively meant tackling *long-term* unemployment – those out of work for six months or a year, or longer. These people are more likely to be victims of the benefits trap. But they also have less chance of finding a job anyway. Employers are more reluctant to recruit people who have been out of work for some time. And the long-term unemployed find it harder to look for work, to prepare for job interviews and to be motivated. These explanations may sound unconvincing: after all, how difficult is it to prepare for a job interview? But research in several industrial countries shows pretty conclusively that these are critical factors.

The supply side

By the 1980s it was clear not only that demand management could do little to help the long-term unemployed in particular, but that the benefits system was structured in a way least likely to help those genuinely looking for work. Major structural problems with the British labour market were also apparent. Even when unemployment was still between two and three million in the early 1980s, skill shortages re-emerged in key sectors of the economy. In other words, some at least of the high levels of unemployment was due to an untrained or insufficiently well trained or educated workforce: there was a mismatch between the demand for and available supply of labour.

This problem had, of course, been recognised as a structural defect for many years. Policy-makers realised that the labour market was insufficiently flexible and adaptable to enable the economy to grow at rates which would in other respects have been desirable. Whenever the British economy grew above its long-term average rate of growth of around 2.25 per cent (known as the *trend* growth rate), inflationary pressures started to build up. This happened because wage rates tended to rise as employers bid for the skilled workers in short supply (and as trade unions sought to maintain pay differentials between different groups of workers). It was a basic illustration of what happens when supply and demand are not in balance.

But it was only in the 1980s, after the Thatcher government had come to power, that there was a systematic attempt to tackle what became known as the supply side of the economy. As we have seen in earlier chapters, the Thatcher administration was vehemently opposed to the idea of manipulating demand to deal with unemployment and, indeed, the Labour government before it had to a large extent moved away from the approach. Now, though, explicit attempts were made to ensure that the labour market – the supply side – responded more flexibly to the demand side.

The supply-side approach involved tackling several problems simultaneously. In the 1970s, Europe – including the UK – had been puzzled by the ability of the US economy to create jobs on an impressive scale. In a period when the economies of the European Community were losing jobs, the US, an economic entity of roughly comparable size and population, was creating them on roughly the same scale. Endless meetings of European economists and policy-makers (at some of which this author was present) were devoted to trying to discover why this should be, in order to benefit from the American experience. The more flexible labour markets of the US were thought to be a key factor.

Flexible labour market policies

There are huge structural differences between the US and the European economies, and it is therefore not easy to replicate the gains of one in the other. But from the 1980s onwards, successive British governments have tried to benefit from the US experience by adopting its labour market policies, which have often been in sharp contrast to those elsewhere in Europe. The British labour market has been deregulated to a much greater extent than in France or Germany, for example. It became easier for employers to take on staff on a temporary or short-term basis; to lay off workers if a company ran into difficulties; to pay lower hourly wages; to employ staff who were not union members and, indeed, to refuse to recognise trade unions. At the same time, the benefit rules were progressively tightened to make it more difficult for those looking for work to refuse jobs which were offered to them, and to oblige them to go on training courses if they lacked adequate skills.

As in so many other areas of economic policy, by the early 1990s a new consensus had begun to emerge – at least among policy-makers linked to the main political parties – about the most appropriate policies to improve the UK's labour market structures and perform-

---

Box 6.1   The Social Chapter

The Social Chapter is actually the Protocol and Agreement on Social Policy annexed to the Treaty on European Union (the Maastricht Treaty), signed in 1991. It is an annex to the Treaty because the UK secured an opt-out during the Maastricht negotiations. Before the 1997 election, however, the Labour Party committed itself to signing the Social Chapter, which it did once elected.

British opposition to the Social Chapter was based on the argument that it would impose unnecessary and costly burdens on employers and would therefore cost jobs. It was seen by its British opponents as creating new restrictions on the labour market because it would give greater rights to employees and therefore reduce labour market flexibility, which was greater in Britain than in other parts of Europe.

The Social Chapter sets out how new EU legislation on some aspects of social and employment policy can be introduced. Measures relating to health and safety, and work and working conditions can be introduced using QMV (see Chapter 4); others, such as social security, need the unanimous agreement of all member states. But, given the objections raised in the UK, what the Social Chapter does not cover is perhaps more important. The minimum wage and trade union legislation are not covered, and there can be no attempt through the Social Chapter to harmonise wage levels across Europe. And the text specifically warns against imposing unnecessary burdens on small businesses.

Among the directives already passed are those concerning parental leave on the birth of a child and on the need for works councils for companies with more than 1,000 employees. Such measures do in theory impose a cost burden on employers, but not a large one. The evidence so far suggests that in practice the impact of the Social Chapter on the UK labour market is likely to be marginal.

ance. Differences of approach began to seem more superficial than substantive. The Labour government which took office in 1997 made relatively few changes to the legal structures governing job security and union membership introduced in the 1980s. It did enter office with a commitment to change the law governing union recognition: but these changes have been substantially watered down from the original aims of the trade union movement.

The Blair government also fulfilled its longstanding promise to sign the Social Chapter of the EU's Maastricht Treaty (see Box 6.1). This, however, seems to have been a classic instance of politicians, as opposed to policy-makers, seeking to exploit and magnify differences between themselves. The Major government had made rejection of the Social Chapter a key element of the 1991 Maastricht negotiations. For the same reason the then Labour opposition had seized on this as a way of presenting themselves in a more pro-European light. The truth is more prosaic: the provisions of the Chapter are unlikely, at least in the short term, to have very much impact on the working lives and rights of most people.

The productivity problem

Unemployment, and the challenge of reducing it, underpinned government efforts to reform labour market structures; but the poor performance of British productivity (see Box 2.3, page 32) strengthened this drive for reform and was seen as an underlying cause of many of the UK's labour market problems. This was an area where, by a wide margin, the UK's performance lagged behind not just that of the US but that of its continental European neighbours. Even in the 1960s this was seen as a critical factor in the UK's relative economic decline. Wage rates rose year after year, but often without any corresponding rise in productivity. Trade unions were often blamed because of their ability to extract pay rises from management. But many economists and policy-makers recognised that poor and weak management was also a major factor. Too many managers had been content to accede to union demands for higher wages without productivity improvements. They had also failed to invest in capital equipment, research and development, and training for their workforces. Those companies which had gone against the trend had succeeded, remaining world leaders in their field: the pharma-ceutical companies are a good example of this. For many other individual companies, their weakness brought disaster. For the British economy as a whole, poor productivity performance brought problems which required radical change in almost every aspect of the labour market.

The trade unions

One of the most fundamental changes concerned the trade unions and the rights of their members. Trade union membership grew steadily throughout the twentieth century, reaching a peak in the late 1970s of about twelve million members, around half the labour force. The leaders of the big unions and the TUC, to which most unions were affiliated, were both powerful and influential; they became more so after the election of the Labour government in 1964, when they were openly courted by ministers. The Labour Party had always had very close ties with unions – the party had its origins as the political wing of the union movement – but union co-operation became increasingly important to Labour and Conservative governments alike as they tried to grapple with the problems of rising inflation and unemployment. Incomes policy could not be implemented effectively without the agreement of the TUC, as both the Heath and Callaghan governments discovered. Strike action organised by the trade unions could cripple the economy: partly because of the willingness of some unions to take extreme action and partly because of the extent and solidarity of trade union membership.

This potential stranglehold on the economy was exercised most visibly in the disputes involving the miners and the electrical power workers in the early 1970s and the 'winter of discontent' of 1978–9, when several public sector unions (including rubbish collectors and gravediggers) went on strike. Many people felt the unions were interested only in advancing their own interests and those of their members: more concerned with pursuing their wage claims than with the damage being done to the national economy through lost output, wage inflation and low productivity growth to which these pay claims and the industrial action in support of them contributed. The Thatcher government came to power determined to get to grips with the problem, in spite of previous failed attempts to curb union power (see Chapter 2). The Thatcher rhetoric was tough, but in practice the new government adopted an incremental approach. The intention was the same, however, and the cumulative effect of the changes was considerable. Unions were obliged to seek proper backing for strike plans by balloting their members; these plans could be challenged in the courts by employers. Secondary picketing – where union members from another company, or even another union, picketed outside a workplace in support of striking workers – was prohibited by law. Closed shops, where all workers at a factory or institution had to be members of a union, were ended.

Changes in the labour market

By the 1990s, union membership had fallen dramatically, to below eight million, barely a third of the workforce. This partly reflected the changing legal environment in which unions had to operate. But it also reflected other changes in the labour market. The privatisation of many of the old state industries, such as telecommunications, gas, electricity, water, steel and coal, also ended their monopoly power and in many cases drastically reduced the workforce involved in the industries. High unemployment itself reduced union membership, as did the changed nature of many people's working lives. More people changed jobs (either from choice or through periods of unemployment). Many industries in which unions had been particularly strong – the car industry, for instance – declined as Britain lost its competitive edge. As foreign investment in the UK grew, it brought new industries and new owners of old industries who were much less tolerant of unions.

The advocates of labour market deregulation argue that these changes brought significant benefits: a substantial rise in productivity growth (although the UK failed to catch up with its competitors) and much lower unemployment in the UK than in continental Europe. The results are certainly evident although, as readers of the earlier chapters will remember, certainty in linking cause and effect in macroeconomic policy can be a mistake. There is, however, another feature of this labour market which many people see as less desirable and which is also attributed to the changes which have been implemented since 1980: the growth of inequality.

Inequality

Inequality, in terms of both income and wealth, is a particularly difficult subject for policy-makers. In a sense, it is right at the heart of

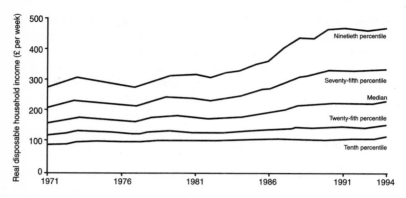

Figure 6.1 Inequality. The graph shows real disposable household income before housing costs for different categories of income earners. The poorest households (the tenth percentile) saw hardly any increase in their real incomes between 1971 and 1994, while the richest (the ninetieth percentile) saw their incomes rise substantially. (Source: Office for National Statistics.)

many political philosophies; it inevitably involves judgement about human nature; and it is also a moral issue. By the end of the twentieth century, politicians had grown less concerned about inequality and less anxious to promote greater equality than their post-war predecessors.

One of the lessons taken from the experience of the welfare state in the past fifty years was the need to avoid making it too difficult for people to strive for improvement by not letting them keep enough of any additional income they earned. This had also been the case put forward against the penal rates of taxation which very high earners faced before 1979 (when they were significantly lowered). Subsequently, policy-makers came to believe it was also desirable to cut standard rates of income tax, so that even people with incomes much closer to the average felt able to benefit. At the same time, the growth in share ownership – through the privatisation of previously nationalised industries and, more recently, through the demutualisation of some building societies and insurance companies and employee savings schemes – has also helped to change the relative wealth distribution.

While politicians may be wary of criticising or even of drawing attention to this change, its significance is something which policy-makers cannot ignore. Figure 6.1 shows that the poorest members of society are now, relative both to the richest and to middle income earners, poorer than they were. Moreover, they are more likely to be unemployed; more likely to have been unemployed for more than a year; and more likely to have few or no skills and educational qualifications. They are classic victims of the benefit trap, caught in poverty from which they seem unable to escape. The social consequences of the existence of this group are debatable: they are seen as one of the factors behind rising crime, for example, although this is an area where it is difficult to find hard evidence. Some, at least, see the existence of such an underprivileged group as morally indefensible, as a challenge to a society which likes to think of itself as civilised. Again, this is difficult territory and beyond the scope of this book.

Skills

But this development of what some commentators have called an underclass has important implications for economic policy. The cost has already been mentioned. Successive governments in the 1990s introduced further modifications to the benefits system to try to curb the soaring social security bill, as well as to improve the incentive and prospects for unemployed people to enter, or re-enter, the workforce. But curbing the costs of welfare is only part of the reason for trying to wean people off benefits. The other is the economic cost which an under-employed workforce represents: lost output. Opinions differ about the actual level of the NAIRU – what we might call the sustainable rate of unemployment; but most economists agree that reducing it involves structural changes which would increase the supply of suitable labour to meet increased demand. People who are on benefit because they cannot find a job or cannot afford to take one are a wasted resource in economic terms. In the long term, the only way to exploit this resource is to create a better-educated and better-trained workforce.

The need for skills is one that has long been recognised, but by the late 1990s the UK had made little progress in tackling the problem. International comparative data show the UK to be among the worst at equipping its workers with suitable skills (see Box 6.2). The UK's record in turning out highly qualified high achievers is among the best in the industrial world. But the record is much less good when it comes to equipping the majority of its population with the education and

---

Box 6.2 Skills

The UK is among the countries with the highest proportion of the population qualified to degree level. But it also has one of the biggest proportions of those educated only to a basic level of literacy. The OECD's International Adult Literacy Survey, carried out between 1995 and 1997, compared seven North American and European countries. In the UK, 23 per cent of the population is educated only to level 1 (the basic literacy level); that compares with only 7 per cent in Germany and Switzerland, which scored best in the survey at this level.

The UK did similarly badly in terms of the proportion of the population qualified to what is known as the intermediate level of literacy skills. Not only was it behind its international competitors at this level, but it also appeared to be falling further behind, as improvements take place at a slower pace than in other countries.

Even more striking was the UK's performance in the Third International Maths and Science Survey, published in 1996. Its thirteen-year-olds did well in science, but came ninth out of ten in maths among children of the advanced industrial countries – only those of the US did worse.

---

skills needed to create a productive workforce. The development of the national curriculum for schools during the 1990s was intended to improve Britain's performance. But confusion continues to surround the debate about intermediate-level skills. Policy-makers have found themselves trying tackle cultural obstacles: the status of engineers in Britain, for example, is significantly lower than in countries such as Germany.

The New Deal

The Blair government took office in 1997 determined to get to grips with some of these problems. Conscious of the criticism levelled at previous attempts to train young people (in particular that they were often devices simply to reduce the unemployment figures), the Labour government introduced the New Deal programme. This was initially aimed at people aged under twenty-five. It presents those unable to find a job with a range of options: a college course; environmental or voluntary work; or a job guaranteed for at least six months by a government subsidy to employers. Claiming benefit is not an option, however. The subsidies paid to employers are controversial, because the scheme's critics believe no new jobs are ever created in this way; they merely displace other workers. In 1998, the scheme was extended to other categories of unemployed workers, although the effectiveness of the scheme will take some time to assess.

The national minimum wage

The Blair government was also responsible for the introduction, in April 1999, of perhaps the most controversial shift in labour market policy in the late twentieth century: a national minimum wage (NMW), the first ever in Britain. On the face of it, this marks the reversal of the shift towards flexible labour market policies pursued by all governments since 1979. The creation of the NMW was one of the few policy commitments made by the Labour Party in opposition and one of even fewer associated with the more traditional egalitarian approach of the party. The drive for it reflected the belief that too many employers were exploiting both their workforce and the welfare system by forcing their employees to rely partly on the relatively limited supplementary benefits available to those in low-paid work. By introducing the NMW, its advocates believed, such exploitation would cease.

The critics of the NMW, however, argued it would not improve standards for workers on very low pay, since most of them would lose their jobs. Employers would not be able to afford to hire as many people if they had to pay them the NMW; either workers would end up working longer hours, or jobs would be lost altogether as some activities became uneconomic. It is significant that, ahead of the introduction of the NMW, academic research suggested that this was unlikely to happen and that some new jobs might even be created as more unemployed people took the view that it was economically worthwhile to take a job. Again, no evidence is yet available as to the impact of the NMW, though the relatively low level chosen (it was fixed at £3.60 in April 1999), coupled with the apparently successful operation of a minimum wage in the US, has eased many fears about the impact – while fostering criticism that it is too low.

The future

Previous chapters have noted the difficulty of assessing the relative importance of the different economic forces at work, and therefore of trying to frame sensible policy. This seems especially true of the labour market. Huge and significant changes have taken place in policies on work and unemployment in the past two decades; others are being introduced at the time of writing. But equally large changes are taking place in patterns of work, both in the UK and in the world economy. These are not directly related to changes in labour market policies, but they do have enormous implications both for the labour market and for macroeconomic policy. They are taking place at great speed – faster than at any time since the beginnings of the Industrial Revolution. It is difficult to keep pace with them, and even more difficult to understand their implications.

Working hours are changing: more people work in the evenings, at night and at weekends; more people – rather ironically – work longer hours. More and more women work. More people work part-time. More people work from home. More are on short-term contracts. At the workplace, how people are managed and remunerated are both changing radically. The fastest-growing occupational sector in the UK is telephone call-centres, where workers are under constant, technological supervision. A small but rapidly growing number of companies encourage worker loyalty and performance by giving them shares or share options in the company. Schemes originally designed for senior executives are now being applied to supermarket shelf-stackers. Even more radical change in patterns of economic activity and thus the labour market result from the spectacular growth of the Internet and the development of e-commerce. Commercial transactions were virtually unknown on the Internet in 1995. Their worldwide growth since then has confounded even the most optimistic forecasts. No one yet knows how this will affect work and working patterns in the twenty-first century, but everyone realises that it will and that these effects will be profound. Yet policy-makers have to try to construct policies which take account of them.

We noted in Chapter 4 that perceptions can be critical in determining the success or otherwise of counter-inflationary policy. This also applies to the labour market. People feel more afraid of losing their job because of the high levels of unemployment in the late 1970s and 1980s. Many people at least knew of someone who had lost their job, even if they themselves were not directly affected. Talk of the end of the 'job for life' increased people's feelings of insecurity. The evidence suggests that, in practice, job tenure has not so far changed as dramatically as people perceive that it has. But the speed of economic change now taking place in the UK and around the world is likely to increase this sense of uncertainty.

7   Fiscal policy and taxation

Fiscal policy has a significant impact on the lives of ordinary people. How much the government spends, and on what; and how that spending is financed – by taxing or borrowing – are all issues of considerable political and economic interest. The annual budget, when the Chancellor announces his tax, spending and borrowing plans for the coming year, is still one of the great events of the political calendar.

What is fiscal policy for?

Yet the second half of the twentieth century was characterised by confusion and controversy about the role of fiscal policy in managing the economy. The post-war period began with the Keynesian revolution, which greatly enhanced the role of fiscal policy. Fifty years later, that view had come to be seen by most policy-makers as irrelevant or mistaken. A new bipartisan consensus had emerged, which placed the emphasis above all on 'sound management of the public finances'.

With hindsight, the confusion is clear. Two things characterised economic management in the period immediately after the Second World War: a belief in a much greater role for the state in the economy; and a belief that fiscal policy could be a vital tool of stabilisation policy. We saw in Chapter 2 how the wartime bargain led to a consensus view that the state had a much larger role in the provision of what might be loosely termed public goods than had previously been accepted. Britain was not alone in moving in that direction: in most industrial countries the state accounted for an increasing proportion of economic activity in the post-war period, though this phenomenon was at times more pronounced in Britain than in many other countries. The consensus, as we saw in previous chapters, had begun to break down by the mid-1970s; but it is important to

136

remember that for all the political rhetoric employed at the time, disagreements were essentially about the extent and degree of government participation at the margin rather than any more fundamental view about the role of the state. There has been no serious attempt, for instance, to remove health care or education as primarily publicly funded activities, nor welfare support as a general principle. Arguments about the extent of provision often centred on the need to prevent the state's involvement from increasing rather than any prolonged or effective efforts to reduce it very significantly. What efforts there were to 'roll back the state', particularly during the Thatcher administration in the 1980s, had only a marginal impact on the core areas of state involvement such as health, education and welfare.

More controversial was the debate over how to fund the state's activity. In a sense, this highlighted the differences of view about the primary purpose of fiscal policy: whether it is to enable the state to redistribute income and wealth; or whether it is to help policy-makers manage the economy by stimulating growth at times of economic downturn and acting to halt excess inflationary pressures caused by boom conditions. Of course, fiscal policy has both these aims, but there is considerable disagreement about their relative political importance.

We saw in earlier chapters the seductive legacy of Keynes's *General Theory*, which many policy-makers interpreted as the green light for very detailed management of demand in the economy. When the private sector failed to generate sufficient activity for cyclical reasons, Keynes believed government-induced investment was a legitimate means of taking up the slack in economic activity and thus boosting demand. But in the post-war period, governments increasingly came to view this role as one which could be conducted on a scale not envisaged by Keynes himself. Small changes in the pace of economic growth were seen as sufficient justification for changing the level of government intervention in the economy. Policy-makers came to think that they could – and therefore should – maintain economic activity at the highest level possible consistent with low inflation, that full employment was an obligation, which they used fiscal policy to meet.

Managing the public finances

Demand management came to play such a prominent role that it tended to obscure the other objective of fiscal policy – managing the public

Table 7.1 The budget deficit: the government's borrowing requirement as a percentage of GDP

Year	%	Year	%
1970–1	-0.6	1985–6	2.3
1971–2	1.0	1986–7	2.1
1972–3	2.9	1987–8	0.9
1973–4	4.5	1988–9	-1.5
1974–5	6.4	1989–90	-0.4
1975–6	7.1	1990–1	0.7
1976–7	5.6	1991–2	3.6
1977–8	4.3	1992–3	7.8
1978–9	4.8	1993–4	7.9
1979–80	3.9	1994–5	6.3
1980–1	4.6	1995–6	4.9
1981–2	2.1	1996–7	3.7
1982–3	3.0	1997–8	1.1
1983–4	3.8	1998–9	-0.1
1984–5	4.2		

Note: a minus figure indicates a surplus.
Data from the Office for National Statistics.

finances. It became too easy for government, anxious to prevent or reverse economic downturn, to let the budget deficit (the amount the government needed to borrow to bridge the gap between spending and tax receipts) rise. It was then a short step to a deficit in danger of spiralling out of control. The more the government borrows, the more interest it has to pay on its debt; and, for a given level of taxing and spending, the more it then has to borrow. This problem became acute in periods of high inflation and high interest rates – in the 1970s, and again, to a lesser extent, in the early 1990s (see Table 7.1).

Moreover, as the financial markets become concerned about the sustainability of the government's fiscal policies, they become more reluctant to lend the government the money it needs to balance its books (see Box 7.1). The government is therefore obliged to pay higher interest rates in order to attract lenders. Falling confidence in the government's ability to manage its finances can also affect the exchange rate if foreign investors decide to shift their money out of sterling.

Box 7.1   How the government borrows money

The government borrows money from its own citizens and anyone else who wishes to lend to it. There are a variety of ways in which it does this:

Treasury bills. These are short-term borrowings from the financial markets which the Bank of England sells on behalf of the Treasury. The bills are sold by auction, which means that the interest rate payable by the government varies: those buyers (i.e. lenders) offering to lend at the lowest rate of interest are those who succeed in their bids.

Gilt-edged securities. These are much longer-term bonds which the Bank of England also sells to a mixture of institutional buyers and individuals – anyone can own gilts, as they are called (their name derives from the fact that the documents were originally gilt-edged). These are usually issued by the government for long periods, of twenty or twenty-five years. They are bearer bonds, which means that they can be bought and sold in the markets and their fixed interest rate is paid to whoever owns them at the time. The interest is paid on the basis that each bond is worth its face value – this is the value at which the government will ultimately redeem it. But they are always traded at a discount, which means that in practice the interest rate is increased. Gilts are also sold initially at auction, again to those bidding the highest price and therefore involving the government in paying the lowest rate of interest it can achieve. The subsequent traded values of gilts reflects other interest rates at the time of the sale.

National Savings. These are both accounts and bonds available for individuals and organised by the Department for National Savings. When the government's borrowing needs are high, interest rates on National Savings tend to be higher than when its borrowing needs are low.

Premium bonds. These bonds – also marketed by the Department for National Savings – pay no interest but are entered into a prize draw every month. The total amount available through the draw equals what would have been paid out in interest if the bonds had been issued in the normal way.

Demand management out of fashion

Government efforts to 'fine-tune' the economy using fiscal policy had become discredited by the 1970s. Although successive Chancellors had sought to make sophisticated adjustments to the level of demand in the economy by using a combination of tax rises or cuts and changes to their spending plans, sharp fluctuations in economic activity continued to plague governments. It became clear that fiscal policy was actually a rather blunt instrument. Tax and spending decisions took a long time to work through and have any impact on demand, by which time they often had the opposite effect of what was intended. By the time the government decided to raise taxes, for instance, in order to slow down an unsustainable boom, the economy might have reached the peak of the cycle. By the time those tax changes took effect, they could therefore be *reinforcing* a fall in demand which was already taking place. The net result might therefore be to exaggerate instead of reduce fluctuations in activity.

These problems came to a head in the 1970s. Faced with rapidly rising unemployment, the Heath government threw caution to the winds in 1971 and injected a massive stimulus into the economy. The economy promptly responded by expanding at an unprecedented rate. But while the fall in unemployment was not as great as had been hoped, government borrowing and inflation both rose sharply. The Labour government came to power in 1974 committed to ambitious public spending plans, which it proceeded to implement until, by 1976, it had become clear that the level of government spending and borrowing had become unsustainable, and help had to be sought from the IMF (as described in Chapters 2 and 3). The lessons learned from the failures of economic management during this period were twofold. First was the need to keep control of the public finances – it was easy for the government's borrowing needs to rise rapidly and unsustainably. Second, demand management did not seem to work: certainly it had failed to check the rise in unemployment during the 1970s while at the same time inflation had also risen to record levels. It was a period of unprecedented economic instability. As it turned out, however, the impact of these lessons faded with time.

Margaret Thatcher appeared to have taken them completely to heart. She took the view that the principal role of fiscal policy was to manage the public finances responsibly. She was often mocked for what critics derided as her housewife's approach to economics: her repeatedly expressed view that governments should not spend more than they could afford and should not seek to borrow large sums to finance their profligacy. Her government sought to curb inflation as its main priority: it argued that low inflation was the prerequisite for economic stability. Thatcher wanted to reduce both the role of the state in the economy and expectations about what state intervention could deliver.

She was also determined to cut government borrowing, and for two years, 1988–90, there was a government surplus. But neither she nor her successor succeeded in rolling back the frontiers of the state to any significant extent or in eliminating budget deficits. Indeed, it could be argued that the economic policy errors made during the latter part of Thatcher's premiership, which led to another bout of high inflation and another severe recession, were in large part the source of the huge budget deficits of the early 1990s.

A new consensus

The very high levels of public borrowing which the Major government faced from 1992 onwards (post-war records in cash terms) made policy-makers determined to set the public finances on a more sound footing. John Major left the public finances in better shape than they had been for many years, with a rapidly falling budget deficit and tighter control of public spending.

By the end of the 1990s a new consensus about the role of fiscal policy had emerged. The Labour government led by Tony Blair chose to build on the Conservative legacy by setting out clear aims for fiscal policy. It was seen as having a more flexible role in helping achieve economic stability. But the Labour government also committed itself to balancing the current budget (current spending and tax receipts) on average over the economic cycle and to stabilise the ratio of government debt to GDP. The latter had been a commitment made by both the Major and Blair governments when they pledged themselves to meet the Maastricht criteria for joining the single European currency (see Box 4.5, page 95): the two main fiscal policy criteria were total government debt limited to 60 per cent of GDP and a budget deficit of no more than 3 per cent of GDP in any one year.

Current versus capital spending

Both the Major and the Blair governments also sought to clarify the distinction between current and capital spending. This is a distinction which commercial enterprises would see as standard. They would never seek to borrow money to finance the running of their day-to-day business: only for investment in new plant or machinery. But the distinction had become blurred in the government's accounts. The old 'golden rule', which prohibited governments from borrowing for current spending, had been largely ignored from the 1970s onwards. Governments borrowed simply to balance their books. The distinction between current spending – on recurrent items such as teachers' salaries, benefit payments and the maintenance of hospitals – and capital spending – new roads, schools and hospitals – was no longer made in practice. In some cases, when public spending cuts were made in a hurry, at times of financial panic, governments found it easier to cut back on plans for capital rather than current spending. This happened on several occasions during the Labour government of 1974–9.

Gordon Brown, who became Chancellor in 1997, committed the government to balance current spending and receipts and to borrow only for new capital investment. The arguments for such a rule in the public sector are partly a matter of good financial management. But there is also a philosophical argument which maintains that current spending which benefits people now should be financed by current taxpayers, and not the taxpayers of future generations (whose taxes would partly go towards repaying government debt); similarly it is legitimate to ask future taxpayers to help pay for a capital investment from which they will benefit.

Problems of implementation

The new approach articulated by the Blair government in the late 1990s was intended to overcome some of the problems of the operation of fiscal policy which had contributed to some of the policy failures of the post-war period. But although these problems are now more clearly recognised, it is difficult to eliminate them altogether. The most important is one of the most serious obstacles to policy-making in the economic sphere: the difficulty of finding out what is actually happening in the economy when policy is being formulated. We saw in Chapter 5 the scale of the problem facing those trying to establish a sensible and feasible counter-inflationary policy. The uncertainties surrounding fiscal policy are at least as great.

Measuring economic activity is difficult and, although statisticians do not like to admit it, it involves a good deal of guesswork. No data on the economy can be wholly accurate: but as a general rule, greater accuracy comes with time. Those responsible for collecting statistics can make more sense of the data and produce more accurate figures the longer they have to analyse the material: hence the number of revisions, some of them significant and substantial, to important data such as GDP and unemployment and earnings figures. But policy-makers' needs are exactly the opposite of the statisticians'. They need information at the earliest opportunity. If you are trying to work out whether the economy is in recession or heading for an upturn, you need to know as soon as possible – the information you seek could be the basis for far-reaching decisions.

Examples of this conflict abound. In 1976, the Labour government had to agree to substantial – and very unpopular – cuts in its spending and borrowing plans in order to secure a balance-of-payments loan from the IMF. These cuts were imposed on the basis of forecasts which turned out to be wrong, by quite substantial margins. The new system of cash limits on public spending had been more effective than ministers and officials realised at the time, and government borrowing was not so high as had been feared. But by the time the correct figures had become available, the new policy commitments had been made, and spending cuts imposed.

In the boom of the late 1980s, the policy-makers got it spectacularly wrong again. The Chancellor, Nigel Lawson, claimed in his March 1988 budget speech that the British economy had been transformed. He based his budget on this assessment, cutting taxes and helping fuel a boom which, with hindsight, was already unsustainable and uncontrollable. Within six months interest rates had been raised to near-record levels in order to curb inflation. The recession of 1990–2 followed.

For all the advances made in economics and econometrics, finding out for certain what is happening in the economy, let alone making an accurate forecast of what will happen, is still close to impossible on a timescale which meets the needs of policy-makers. So it is difficult to assess the situation at the time and respond to it. It is equally difficult to set a policy objective and be sure of achieving it. In the 1981 budget, the Chancellor, Sir Geoffrey Howe, sought – deliberately – to tighten fiscal policy (i.e. reduce government borrowing and increase taxation) during a recession. This was seen as a very severe move and was intended to indicate the government's determination to bring both inflation and the government's finances under control. In the event, the figures subsequently showed that the fiscal stance was actually relaxed in the budget, because the government's assessment of the situation and its forecast were both wrong. Equally, successive attempts to bring government borrowing under control from 1992 onwards were less successful than anticipated, because the outturn figures showed that the government ended up borrowing more than it planned.

The cyclical problem

The cyclical behaviour of the economy adds to the difficulty of economic assessment and forecasting. Economies tend to run in cycles, sometimes known as the business cycle. Typically, demand will gradually rise over several years, as GDP grows at a gradually increasing rate; and then demand starts to fall and the rate of GDP growth slows down. In extreme cases, the slowdown will turn into a recession, when GDP actually shrinks. (The official definition of a recession is three successive quarters of negative GDP growth.) It is these cycles which governments in the first decades after the Second World War thought they could smooth out or eliminate by using fiscal policy, or demand management. We saw in Chapters 1 and 2 that this ambition was abandoned by policy-makers after the experience of the 1970s.

But cyclical problems have not disappeared, nor has the desire of policy-makers to respond to them. Politicians do not want to preside over recessions. They are painful for those worst affected, who may lose their jobs or see their businesses fail. They are also electorally very unpopular – they cost votes. Economists see cyclical fluctuations as undesirable because of the waste of resources they represent. Large numbers of people unemployed or large amounts of under-utilised capital in the form of factories or machinery lying empty or idle mean the economy is not being used to full capacity. Recessions help create or add to what is known as the output gap: the gap between the level of GDP which is actually reached and that which would have been reached if the economy had grown at its long-term average rate. Economists and policy-makers would therefore like to see the economy growing much more steadily, at a rate which can be sustained over a long period.

This does not sound such an ambitious aim: but it is. In the first place, not enough is known about why economies are subject to cyclical fluctuations. It is difficult, therefore, to know precisely what policy action would help minimise them. As we have seen, it is also difficult simply to detect accurately what is going on in the economy at any particular time. It is hard enough to be sure that, for example, the economy is turning down (i.e. GDP growth is slowing); and even harder to know whether that slowdown is cyclical, or whether it represents some structural change in the economy which could alter its long-term growth potential.

Governments want to improve the growth performance of the economy. They want high and stable growth rates. They tend to be eager, therefore, to attribute apparent changes in the economy to structural rather than cyclical factors. This was partly responsible for Nigel Lawson's over-optimism in 1988. The economic forecasts were wrong and unduly optimistic, but Lawson was predisposed to believe them. Similarly, when the government's budget deficit turned into a surplus in 1987, the government was adamant that this represented a structural shift. It was, in fact, simply a reflection of the buoyant state of the economy and tax revenues – the reversal into deficit was sudden and exceptionally steep. For that reason, some observers were inclined to treat the Blair government's optimistic assessment of its ability permanently to reduce government borrowing and balance the budget over the cycle with some caution, if not scepticism. Although the upswing of the late 1990s was unusually prolonged, a much longer time-span would be needed to determine the extent to which cyclical fluctuations had been significantly reduced, with all the favourable implications which this would have for the control of government borrowing. A severe recession, for instance, while an apparently unlikely prospect at the beginning of the twenty-first century, could make the government seem overly ambitious and damage its credibility.

Credibility

Failure to meet targets for public borrowing always undermines a government's credibility to some extent. Sceptics would argue that the government never really intended to achieve them. This might be true in some cases – such figures and forecasts are easy to fudge. But simply getting the outcome wrong is also perfectly plausible, as we have seen. So many factors are involved. It is important to remember, above all, that the budget deficit is the relatively small difference between two very large numbers. Take the outturn figures for 1997–8, for example. The government's current spending was over £300 billion, and so were tax receipts. The deficit was £5 billion – less than 2 per cent of these sums. This is a very small difference, when we consider what fluctuations can occur on both sides of the equation. Any rise in unemployment would lead to more benefit payments being made; it would also mean fewer income tax receipts. Tax receipts could also be affected by a drop-off in business activity, which would reduce the tax take from companies and from VAT. Higher interest rates could lead to higher debt payments.

Impact and intent

We have seen that the use of fiscal policy as a tool to manage demand in the economy has largely been discredited. But it is important to distinguish between this and the recognition that fiscal policy can affect demand. Both fiscal and monetary policy can have a major impact on demand – we saw in Chapter 5 that high interest rates had in effect been used to squeeze demand out of the economy, causing both the 1980–1 and 1990–2 recessions. The problem with using fiscal policy to squeeze demand – raising taxes sharply, for example – is not that it has no impact but that the nature and speed of its impact are unpredictable. The economy has been likened to a supertanker. The captain of a supertanker knows that to change course the signal to do so must be given long before the change needs to take place – the vessel is so large that it can respond only slowly to such signals. The problem for the economy's captain – the Chancellor – is that he does not have enough advance warning of the need to change course to do so accurately and effectively.

Tax policy – a radical shift

The shift in the consensus on fiscal policy coincided with a major change in attitudes to taxation. From 1945, governments of both parties had presided over a rise in the tax burden (the share of GDP paid in taxes) – which was inevitable because of the growth in public spending over that period. But taxation had itself been part of the armoury of demand management. Income tax had been raised or lowered according to the perceived excess or shortfall of demand; sales taxes (purchase tax up to 1973, VAT thereafter) had been used in a similar fashion.

Margaret Thatcher was committed to radical tax reform. She wanted to lower the overall tax burden – an objective consistent with her desire to reduce the role of the state in the economy. She wanted to leave people with more of their income, free to decide for themselves whether to spend or save it. She was keen to bring down the higher rates of income tax as fast as possible – she saw these penal rates as a disincentive to enterprise and entrepreneurship – but she also wanted to reduce the standard rates of income tax. Her government also favoured a shift from income tax to sales taxes as part of the philosophy of letting people choose what to do with their money.

Her first Chancellor, Sir Geoffrey Howe, made an impressive start on these reforms in his first budget in June 1979. The highest rate of income tax came down from 83 per cent to 60 per cent, the standard rate from 33 per cent to 30 per cent. VAT rose from 8 per cent to 15 per cent. These changes were highly controversial. The Labour opposition was vehemently opposed to the rise in VAT, but above all to the cut in higher-rate income tax. They were equally strongly opposed to the subsequent cut in higher-rate tax to 40 per cent in Nigel Lawson's 1988 budget.

It nevertheless became clear during the 1980s that income tax cuts were politically popular. Arguments that income taxes needed to be raised to pay for under-funded public services fell on deaf ears, at least in electoral terms. Public opinion polls suggested that people would be willing to pay more tax to fund an increase in health or education spending: but in elections they consistently voted for those politicians who promised further tax cuts. A major contributing factor in Labour's defeat in the 1992 election was reckoned to be the shadow budget, presented by John Smith during the election campaign. He set out what he would do if Chancellor; crucially, his plans included raising taxes on middle-income earners – those whose votes Labour needed to win.

During the course of the 1990s, therefore, Labour followed the Conservatives by moving decisively in favour of lower rates of income tax. Each party tried to out-do the other with promises of future reductions. The Conservatives introduced a lower rate of income tax (20 per cent) on the first few thousand pounds of taxable income. In 1999, the Labour Chancellor, Gordon Brown, committed himself to a new band of 10 per cent, to be introduced from 2000. It seems inconceivable that any party could win power by promising to raise taxes.

Smoke and mirrors

Income tax cuts were popular, but not so generous as they first appeared. The overall tax burden on the economy did not fall during the eighteen years of Conservative government, for example (see Table 7.2). In 1981, for instance, the government actually increased the total amount of tax people paid. And while Chancellors enjoy the headlines they get from cutting income tax *rates*, such reductions do not benefit the less well off members of society as much as other changes would. It is much more effective to help the poor by raising tax *thresholds* – the amount which can be earned before tax liability starts. Raising the basic-rate threshold by more than the rate of inflation will mean that hundreds of thousands of people immediately stop paying tax at all. But such changes are expensive; their significance is harder to explain to the public; and they generate far fewer headlines than rate cuts.

Such tax reforms have implications for fiscal policy. The pledges which politicians now make, to keep income tax rates low and falling, inevitably constrain policy-makers. An unexpected fall in tax revenues or a surge in spending can no longer be met by higher taxes (nor by government borrowing – see above). The burden has to fall on the spending side of the equation.

Table 7.2   The tax burden: net taxes and social security contributions as a percentage of GDP

Year	%	Year	%
1978–9	33.3	1989–90	36.2
1979–80	34.1	1990–1	36.3
1980–1	35.8	1991–2	35.2
1981–2	38.9	1992–3	33.9
1982–3	39.1	1993–4	33.2
1983–4	38.4	1994–5	34.3
1984–5	39.0	1995–6	35.2
1985–6	38.2	1996–7	35.4
1986–7	37.8	1997–8	36.6
1987–8	37.7	1998–9	37.2
1988–9	36.8		

Data from the Office for National Statistics.

Globalisation

These constraints are partly a reflection of globalisation. The political consensus in the UK about lower income tax rates is matched increasingly by an international consensus. In theory, governments remain free to impose whatever tax rates they and their citizens want. In practice their freedom is constrained by the financial markets and because of the greater international competition for economic activity. A tax regime which the markets judged (rightly or wrongly) to be detrimental to the UK's economic prospects could affect international investor confidence, and so the exchange rate. More significantly, in the longer term a high-tax regime could influence both foreign investors considering a move to the UK or encourage companies already in the UK to move their operations elsewhere. The level of taxes on company profits is an important factor in such decisions, as is the level of income taxes, especially on high-earning managers. Policy-makers today have to take account of the international implications of taxation policy to a much greater extent than they used to.

Taxation as an instrument of social policy

For a good part of the post-war period, taxation was also seen as an instrument of social policy, as a means of redistributing income and wealth from the richer members of society to the poor. This was one of the motivations, for example, behind the penal rates of income tax – up to 98 per cent on unearned income at one point. But the use of taxation in this way has diminished. High rates of tax were thought to be a disincentive to enterprise and, because of the relatively small sums involved (the tax rates were high but there were not that many people paying them), the revenue from higher-rate taxpayers did not go very far when redistributed. The political swing in favour of lower income taxes at all levels of income (see above) also restricted the opportunities for governments to develop more progressive systems of taxation, for example by skewing the tax system in favour of the poor by raising tax thresholds. Policy-makers have long been attracted to the idea of using the tax and benefit systems together to help the poor: ideas such as a negative income tax, where non-taxpayers would get some sort of cash benefit from the state, have been canvassed. But the logistical problems from combining the revenue and benefit systems have so far proved too great to overcome.

Box 7.2   Local taxation

Local taxation became a serious problem for policy-makers in the latter part of the twentieth century. Until the 1990s, local tax revenue came from the rates – a property tax dating from 1601, based on a complicated assessment of the rental value of a property (which was linked in turn to its market value). The rateable value of property was assessed at regular intervals by the Inland Revenue, but the tax was collected by local authorities. As house prices rose and rateable values increased, the rates became increasingly unpopular and were widely seen as unfair. The Thatcher government postponed a new valuation exercise because it feared the political backlash.

After much internal wrangling, and opposition from some members of the government, a new local tax, the poll tax (it was officially called the community charge) was introduced, in 1989 in Scotland and in 1990 in England and Wales. It was immediately and hugely unpopular. Although intended to be a fairer tax than the rates, it was in fact regressive in that it was a flat-rate per-person tax and so was much less burdensome on the better off than on the poor, even when rebates for pensioners and those in receipt of social security benefits were taken into account. The unpopularity of the poll tax was widely seen as one of the factors which led to Thatcher's departure from office.

In 1992, the poll tax was replaced with a new local tax, the council tax. This was a reversion to a property-tax system: a charge levied on each property according to its value in a series of bands. Its advantages were simplicity and a greater degree of fairness than the poll tax, although it was still weighted in favour of the better-off. At the same time a new and rather complicated system for raising revenues from businesses was introduced.

The real problem with local taxation was the sharp fall in the local tax base which all three systems represented. As local authority spending (much of it directed by central government) rose sharply, especially from the 1970s onwards, the tax base shrank in relative terms. It was supplemented by a large grant from central government. Locally raised revenue represented more than half of all local government spending in 1979–80: by the time the poll tax was introduced it was below 20 per cent.

Chancellors and their officials love to tinker with the tax system: old taxes are abolished and new ones introduced with surprising frequency. But aside from income tax, VAT and corporation tax, such tinkering is at the margin. Removing some old or anomalous tax is all very well, but at the end of the day the government's books have to balance. For any given budget deficit, the Chancellor has relatively little flexibility: the revenue has to come from somewhere. As resistance to income tax rises has grown, extra revenue, when needed, has had to come from elsewhere. Sometimes this comes from a new tax which the Chancellor decides he can get away with politically, such as the new tax on insurance premiums introduced in 1997.

But in other cases, the need for revenue is combined with a decision by the Chancellor to try to alter people's behaviour by changing the price of some activity. For many years, successive Chancellors raised the excise duty on tobacco, to provide a financial disincentive to smokers. Similarly, in the 1990s, taxes were increased on ordinary petrol and reduced on diesel fuel, to encourage a switch to what was then thought to be a more environmentally acceptable fuel. This was abandoned when new scientific evidence cast doubt on diesel.

Economists tend to disagree about the desirability of using the tax system to try to influence people's behaviour in this way. Some regard it as interfering with the normal mechanism of the market; in an ideal world, they argue, taxes should have a neutral impact on people's behaviour. A tax on insurance premiums, for instance, is criticised as acting as a disincentive to take out insurance. But some economists see fuel taxes, for example, as a legitimate means of shifting people's behaviour precisely because it alters the balance of the decision about whether to use more or less petrol by using the price mechanism rather than any kind of rationing.

Savings

The tax treatment of savings is perhaps the most controversial of taxes designed to affect people's behaviour. Governments generally are keen to encourage savings rather than consumption: savings can be used for investment in economic output, whereas consumption by individuals often takes the form of purchasing imports. Consumption can add to inflationary pressures and can worsen the balance-of-payments situation – both persistent problems for the UK economy in the post-war period. One way to encourage savings is to offer tax breaks for people willing to save over a longer period. But it can be very difficult to know whether such tax breaks work.

In 1990, the Chancellor, John Major, introduced a new form of savings account (known as a TESSA). If people saved their money in this account for five years the interest they earned was tax free. Critics of the scheme pointed out that it would be impossible to tell what proportion of people benefiting from this account was already intending to save: anyone who would have saved in any case was getting a free handout from the government since the tax break had not altered their behaviour. But the scheme was extended after its first five years, and replaced by a different tax-free scheme (known as ISAs) by the Labour government in 1999. As with so many economic policy decisions, it was not possible for anyone to be sure to what extent the objective of more saving *than would otherwise have taken place* had been achieved.

8 The exchange rate

Defining the policy objectives

Exchange rate policy is perhaps uniquely complicated. For a country such as Britain, which depends heavily on international trade and investment, the level of the exchange rate, as well as its relative stability or volatility, is crucially important. Yet there are wide divergences of view as to what level is desirable and what level of volatility is acceptable. Different sectors of the economy have very different views on these matters, as do policy-makers themselves. Moreover, policy-makers may find themselves not only between competing views on the subject, but also between an intellectual and an emotional assessment of policy which is perhaps greater than in any other sphere of economic policy.

If framing sensible objectives for the exchange rate is difficult, constructing a policy which is feasible in execution is pretty much impossible. British economic policy in the twentieth century is littered with failures in this area. At virtually no point has a policy been devised, implemented and judged successful. Even more striking is the extent to which the same misjudgements have been made by a succession of policy-makers. Two devaluations of the pound, in 1949 and 1967, bore marked similarities in the way they were handled. The collapse of the Major government's policy on the ERM in September 1992 had uncanny echoes of the forced abandonment of the Gold Standard which took place under the National Government in September 1931.

Many of the difficulties with exchange rate policy stem from this double ambivalence – of what is desirable and what is sensible. Even the language of exchange rate management reveals this. Currencies are either 'strong' or 'weak', weak being a derogatory term: thus sterling's weakness, a decline in its value against other currencies, which began

Box 8.1   Exchange rates

The exchange rate is the rate at which one currency can be exchanged
for another – for example, three German marks for one pound, or six
French francs for one dollar. Rates can be fixed or floating. If the rate
is fixed, the government concerned has publicly said it will support
that rate: the level of demand for the currency, the number of people
wanting to buy or sell it, will not *in the short term* affect the rate, since
the central bank will be prepared to buy or sell as required. Fixed
rates can be changed, but this is always difficult, partly for political
reasons but also because on a practical level the two governments
concerned have to agree. If fixed currencies are part of a system, more
governments may be involved, making agreement even more complicated.

Since the 1970s, with certain exceptions such as the EMS between
1979 and 1999, most major currencies have been floating. Floating can
take two forms: free and managed (or clean and dirty). Free floating
means the government takes no active role in determining the value of
the currency; managed means that the government seeks to influence
the value, in a number of ways. In both cases government action and
policies will affect the exchange rate.

Currency values are determined by a complex range of factors. At
the most basic level they reflect a judgement – made by individuals,
the markets, or both – about the relative worth of one currency compared with another. This will take into account: the purchasing power
of a currency in its home market and, linked to this, the level of
inflation; the flows of money between countries resulting from trade
and investment activity; relative interest rates; and speculative financial
flows. Speculative financial flows are perhaps the most important in
their direct impact on the pressure for changes in currency values,
although it is important to remember that such flows can reflect
judgements about other factors, such as the inflation prospects for a
country.

Governments which want to intervene to influence the exchange rate
can do so directly – by buying or selling their own currency, or that of
other countries. They can also try to influence flows by domestic policy
changes – interest rate adjustments, or changes to counter-inflationary
policy, which may make their currency more or less attractive to foreign
investors.

in 1931 and has continued with few interruptions since 1945, is seen as
an indication of policy failure. Currency strength or weakness is seen
as a symbol of national achievement and a source of pride or shame.
No other economic indicator carries with it the ability to assume the
role of national identity. Yet if the decline in the external value of a
currency is a weakness, it is because of policy failures elsewhere in the
economy, most notably the failure to keep domestic inflation rates low
in comparison with those elsewhere. The long-term decline in sterling
is seen as a proxy for Britain's economic decline (in contrast to the
prolonged weakness of the American dollar, which is not seen as
reflecting the state of the US economy). It is difficult to separate such
perceptions from efforts to construct a policy for exchange rate
management.

Developing a policy

There are those who argue that any effort to develop an exchange rate
policy is fundamentally mistaken: that the exchange rate should be
seen as a residual, its level determined by market forces, which are
best able to assess the value of any one currency against another. There
are two flaws in this view. The first is something that all governments
learn sooner or later: no policy on the exchange rate can be neutral.
Almost every aspect of economic policy (and sometimes other policies
as well) has an impact on the exchange rate, whether intended or not.
The second mistake is to assume that foreign exchange markets are
omniscient. Most market operators would concede that financial
markets frequently overreact; the herd instinct in markets is highly
developed and extreme judgements on the exchange rate can quickly
be reversed without any sign of a change in economic fundamentals.
If, for example, sterling is worth \$1.63 one day and \$1.66 the next, it
may tell us nothing about UK economic growth or inflation, or unemployment. But such a change would be of considerable importance to
some British businesses. Exporters would suddenly find that, for a
given dollar price, any goods they were to sell in the US would bring
in about 2 per cent less revenue when converted to sterling. This
might sound like an insignificant change, but it could be critical for
businesses operating on narrow margins in a very competitive environment. Exchange rate swings of this kind are not uncommon even over
the course of a day. It is, above all, the economic impact of any given

level of the exchange rate, and changes in it, which makes it both imperative to have an exchange rate policy and, simultaneously, impossible to have one which meets with anything approaching universal approval.

Putting policy into practice

The gap between policy and its successful execution is substantial. The Bretton Woods system of managed exchanged rates, introduced after the war with the central participation of Britain (see Box 8.2), predated the highly mobile capital markets which came to dominate the international financial system from the 1980s onwards and which make policy implementation so difficult nowadays. Nevertheless, the Bretton Woods era was characterised by growing tensions which twice forced a British government to devalue the pound against its will (in 1949 and 1967). That these were both Labour governments had important economic policy implications because of the political impact they had on policy-makers across the political spectrum. At that time, stability of the exchange rate was seen as vital, partly because of the substantial holdings of sterling-denominated assets by foreign governments and others (these holdings were known as the sterling balances). Devaluation inevitably meant other holders of pounds suddenly found their assets worth less: this itself had consequences for the political relationship between Britain and these holders. It also made the UK more vulnerable in the 1970s to switches out of sterling into assets denominated in other currencies, which in turn affected the exchange rate.

Bretton Woods collapsed in 1971 as a result of American policy and sterling, like most major currencies, floated for most of the 1970s and 1980s. But policy in the 1970s once again reflected the ambivalence of policy-makers. We saw in Chapter 1 that, in 1972, the UK briefly joined the snake, a European attempt to stabilise several currencies against the US dollar by linking them together and intervening in the foreign exchange markets to support each currency within a specified narrow band. Britain's participation lasted six weeks before the government was forced to withdraw the pound because of overwhelming market pressure: the reserves had been depleted by $2.6 billion. Policy was rapidly reversed as policy-makers within the Treasury who favoured a significant depreciation of sterling to make exports more competitive carried the day. But this policy, too, proved to have unpalatable

---

Box 8.2   The Bretton Woods system

Following what was seen as the failure of international monetary and trade co-operation in the 1930s, the US and the UK sought to establish a new international economic framework after the war. Negotiations took place during the war, and ended with the Bretton Woods agreement of 1944 (see Chapter 1). Two of the key aims were to ensure international monetary stability and to provide sufficient international liquidity, that is, enough money in the world system to finance economic growth.

The Bretton Woods exchange rate system was known as the fixed but adjustable peg. Each currency was fixed by reference to its value in July 1944 (with a one-off change of up to 10 per cent permitted). Governments were obliged to keep their currency's value within 1 per cent either side of that rate.

These rates could be changed, but this had to be negotiated and agreed by all the participants – a complex process.

At the core of the new system was the US dollar, which became the world's monetary anchor. The US government committed itself to exchanging dollars for gold at the rate of $35 per ounce. There was a dollar shortage after the war: people needed dollars to buy American products, but because the US did not import so much from other countries, there were not enough dollars available outside the US for this purpose. Because of this, most currencies were not freely convertible until 1958 – they could not automatically be converted into dollars or any other currency.

The Bretton Woods system finally collapsed in 1971, when the US government closed the 'gold window' (i.e. refused to convert dollars into gold).

---

consequences. Britain's longstanding propensity to import meant that the greatest impact of the falling pound was on inflation, as import prices soared.

A similar seesaw pattern emerged in the 1980s. The Thatcher government, or at least the Prime Minister herself, was at first inclined to the view that a strong pound was politically desirable. Sharply rising interest rates (aimed at curbing inflation) coupled with confidence in a new government determined to deal with inflation saw the pound soar, adding to the tight squeeze on the economy then manifesting itself in the sharpest recession since the war. By 1982 sterling was once more losing value and this was largely responsible for the substantial economic recovery seen at that time. By January 1985, the Prime

Minister was alleged to be happy with the idea of the pound at parity with the dollar – a story which sparked hysteria in the foreign exchange markets and led to a rise in interest rates of 3.5 per cent in less than three weeks.

The pound and macroeconomic policy: the ERM

The early 1980s brought home to policy-makers, even if they did not want to admit it, how important the exchange rate could be as a tool of macroeconomic management. By the mid-1980s, some policy-makers, at official and ministerial level, had become increasingly convinced that the exchange rate could be a useful weapon in the fight against inflation. Their judgement was based on the experience of those countries which had been members of the ERM since its inception in 1979. The German mark was the anchor of the system; and the mark enjoyed an unparalleled reputation as a hard currency – that is, one unlikely to lose its value – as a result of the persistently tough anti-inflationary policy of the German Bundesbank. As a result, the other currencies in the system had enjoyed a remarkable degree of stability in relation to each other (though not necessarily to currencies outside the system, such as the US dollar and the Japanese yen). These countries generally had also made significantly more progress in fighting inflation than had the UK. Given the failure of monetary control as a counter-inflationary tool (see Chapter 5), ERM membership seemed an attractive alternative to some members of the government. Thatcher, however, vetoed the idea in 1985. We saw in Chapter 2 that this did not stop Chancellor Nigel Lawson from shadowing the mark secretly in 1987–8; and we noted in Chapter 5 the consequences this had for the government's policy on inflation.

It is important to note, too, the lessons which this experience once again offered policy-makers tempted to target the exchange rate. Lawson settled on a rate of one pound for three marks as his target. His problems with inflation stemmed from the fact that the financial markets tended to push sterling above this level over a period of months. Lawson's solution was to cut interest rates when this happened: this acted as a check on foreign investors, since each interest rate cut reduced the return they were able to get on their sterling assets. But in focusing on the exchange rate, the Chancellor failed to pay sufficient attention to the domestic consequences of his policy. It would be wrong, however, to infer from this that Lawson was alone in his misjudgements. We saw in Chapters 2 and 4 the events that led up to the UK joining the ERM on 8 October 1990. Barely a year later, this move had become controversial in both political and economic terms as the extent and nature of its impact became clear. But at the time of entry, the judgements made were overwhelmingly favourable, not least from industry, which believed exchange rate stability coupled with falling inflation to be a decisive combination. In the first few months of British ERM membership, this judgement appeared to be correct. Sterling remained stable and the government was able to make a series of cuts in interest rates without affecting that stability. But as interest rates tightened around Europe following German reunification, and as market pressure grew for similar rises in the UK, the price of ERM membership became unpopular. With the British recession showing no signs of easing, the idea of interest rate rises – both before and after the general election of May 1992 – seemed unthinkable. Yet without those interest rate rises, sterling's position within the ERM came under increasing strain.

The ERM is an uncomfortable illustration of the extent to which even experienced economists and policy-makers can make serious mistakes about exchange rate policy. Ahead of British membership of the ERM, the most widely held fear was that upward pressure on sterling would prove too great and that premature cuts in interest rates would prove necessary to halt sterling's rise – a repetition of the problems encountered in 1988 when interest rate reductions had helped fuel inflation. In fact, the opposite problem soon proved to be the case. This was politically far more difficult since, whatever their economic consequences, interest rate cuts tend to be popular; interest rate rises never are.

With hindsight, it is clear that by mid-1992 sterling's position had become unsustainable in the absence of interest rate rises much earlier than those finally imposed on 16 September, and that even they might have failed to stabilise the currency. By the time the pound was forced out of the ERM – along with the lira – the size of market speculation against sterling was overwhelming and unprecedented in scale.

Analysis of a crisis

The objectives in joining the ERM were essentially twofold, although there is good reason to suspect that Thatcher, the Prime Minister at the time of entry, had a third in mind. She was persuaded by her Chancellor (shortly afterwards her successor) that only by joining the ERM could he deliver the interest rate cut that she wanted, for political reasons, ahead of the Conservative Party's annual conference the following week. Ostensibly, though, ERM membership would in economic terms reinforce government efforts to reduce and then control inflation; and in political terms, it would make clear to the UK's European partners its renewed commitment to the EU. Industry and most (though not all) opinion formers were in favour of ERM entry, though not always for the same reasons. Industry wanted a stable exchange rate, lower interest rates and lower inflation. There were hopes that the ERM would deliver these.

But industry in general gradually changed its view of the ERM and it is instructive to see why. The ERM did not offer stability to the pound; it merely reduced the scope for fluctuations against other currencies in the system (see Box 2.5, page 48). It could not prevent fluctuations between ERM currencies and third currencies like the dollar or the yen – movement in both of which is a major source of international currency market volatility. About 40 per cent of the UK's trade was with countries outside the ERM zone. Moreover, even the fluctuations permitted within the ERM bands were substantial: because of sterling's wider bands it could, in theory, move by up to 12 per cent from the top to the bottom of its band, and vice versa.

As sterling's position within the system came under pressure, it moved towards the lower end of its band, and the challenge for the authorities was to ensure it stayed above the minimum level without having to raise interest rates. It could be argued that this decline should have been welcome to industry since it made British exports more competitive, if only by a relatively small amount. But as the effects of the ERM began to bite, industry had two complaints: one was the level of interest rates, which remained uncomfortably high at a time of moderately severe recession; the other was the entry level of sterling. Gone were the days when businesses could have hoped for some relief from competitive pressures via a depreciating pound. ERM membership held out the prospect of lower inflation. It also meant a continuing challenge for the domestic economy to become more competitive by, for example, increasing productivity; sterling would no longer adjust to make life easier for those exporting companies not as efficient as their overseas competitors. So arguments mounted about whether sterling had gone into the ERM at the appropriate level.

These arguments neatly illustrate the impossibility of finding an exchange rate policy to suit everyone. By the winter of 1991–2, the original concerns about sterling's entry level – that it would be in danger of breaching the *upper* bands – had been forgotten. Now critics argued that instead of a central rate of DM2.95 the pound should have entered at something nearer to DM2.75 or even DM2.60. This argument failed to take into account the situation at the time of entry and subsequently. It was simply an argument of hindsight.

More significantly, this view also failed to take account of the reality facing policy-makers at the time. Currencies joining the ERM could not unilaterally choose their own rate: entry had to be negotiated with the other member countries. The UK had, indeed, technically breached proprieties by announcing (on 5 October) the rate at which sterling would join, ahead of negotiations. These took place over the weekend before the pound formally joined on 8 October. At those negotiations, British officials did in fact have some leeway: they could have *raised* the entry rate to DM2.96 or DM2.97. They had no authority to agree to a lower rate, however, and even if they had it would have been of little use. Although the German negotiators were concerned that the entry level for sterling was on the high side, others – notably the French and the Italians – were pressing for a higher entry rate.

The importance of unpredictable events

The ERM episode is instructive in another way. Although the pound was under some pressure from late 1991, this was erratic; sterling only gently drifted below its central rate. The recession in the UK had been more persistent than anyone had forecast, and the consequences of ERM membership became increasingly unpopular (though the policy of membership went largely unchallenged). The crucial turning point for sterling was a series of political developments entirely outside the UK and of apparently little relevance to the operation of the ERM. The financial markets became seriously unsettled when, in early June 1992, the Danish electorate voted against the ratification of the Maastricht Treaty in a referendum. Since the central element of the Treaty was the plan for EMU, the markets interpreted this as a sign that the EMU project was in trouble (see pages 110–11). These anxieties were compounded when President Mitterrand immediately announced that there would be a referendum in France, too. The summer of acute turbulence reflected political uncertainties about the future of the single-currency project, which caused foreign exchange traders to reassess their analysis of the future of the ERM currency parities. Turbulence became something closer to market panic when opinion polls showed that the French might also vote against the Maastricht Treaty in the referendum set for September. On 20 September they voted in favour by the narrowest of majorities.

As is so often the case with exchange rate problems, sterling was caught in the wake of the turbulence which had its origins elsewhere. Even though there was, even then, no prospect of the pound being part of the first wave of currencies joining EMU, the political crisis had focused attention on sterling, as well as on the lira and the peseta: because these were seen as the weakest currencies in the ERM. In the case of sterling, too, the persistence of the recession had made it clear that the government was extremely reluctant to raise interest rates. Its statements about the strength of the commitment to stay in the ERM and not to devalue sounded less and less credible when not accompanied by action to support these assertions.

Policy and the markets

Having a clear policy on the exchange rate can cause more trouble than it is worth. If the policy is challenged, the policy-maker then has to decide how best to respond. This is not a straightforward decision: market psychology as well as economics is involved. Markets will often test a target or a fixed rate, in order to see how easily the authorities can be shifted. This may be because traders or investors think a particular rate implausible on economic grounds. But it may not be. It may even be that movement in an exchange rate has more to do with other currencies. The pound could rise or fall against the US dollar, for example, but this could have much more to do with changing market sentiment about the dollar and the US economy than with market views of sterling. In theory, of course, any shift says something about the relative merits of whichever two currencies are being traded. In practice this is far from always the case. As we noted earlier, markets often overshoot in one direction or another. Since policy-makers have to deal with reality, not theory, judging the appropriate policy response can be difficult. Pursuing what may be considered the most desirable policy can sometimes be impossible.

Take the example already mentioned (on pages 157–8), that of the market pressure on sterling in January 1985 – long before the UK joined the ERM. If a currency declines for whatever reason and the authorities want to halt or reverse that decline, there are two obvious short-term responses. One is for the authorities (the Bank of England acting on instruction from the Treasury) to intervene in the foreign exchange market: by using the reserves to buy pounds they would hope to push up its value. But given the huge scale of foreign currency trading (something like $400 billion or more every day in London alone), intervention is now of limited value.

The other short-term option is to raise interest rates. If a currency declines, it means another has risen; at its most basic this reflects the fact that more people are selling pounds, say, than buying them. Raising interest rates should make that currency more attractive to hold because the return on assets denominated in that currency has now increased. At some point, if interest rates are raised far enough, more people will want to buy pounds than to sell them. The pound's value will then rise – a simple demonstration of the laws of supply and demand. In January 1985, the pound started to fall quite sharply against the dollar. This could probably have been halted if the government had made it clear that it did not want to see this fall in value and if it had then raised interest rates accordingly.

Instead of a clear message, however, the Prime Minister's office gave some journalists to understand that she at least was not unhappy with the decline in sterling, and might even be content to see it fall further. Much to the fury of the Chancellor (who had not been consulted and did not share this view) the markets responded by selling pounds on a large scale. Within hours, the value of the pound had fallen so sharply that the government was forced to act to prevent a complete debacle. Interest rates were raised. But in a painful lesson ministers discovered that a large rise – 3.5 percentage points over two weeks – was needed before the markets believed that the government was determined to halt the decline and were persuaded to start buying pounds again. Interest rates had to be raised by far more than would have been necessary if the market had not received such conflicting signals.

Defending a fixed rate is even more difficult, as the ERM crisis demonstrated nearly eight years later. As the government's reluctance to take action – by raising interest rates – became more disturbing for the markets, confusion once more reigned. By 16 September, when traders sold pounds on an unprecedented scale, the interest rate option was no longer viable. A 5 per cent rise in interest rates announced in two stages, two hours apart, did nothing to stop people selling sterling. These were regarded as too late; they were also seen as counter-productive because of the potential damage they would inflict on the economy, already weak. In the event, as sterling left the ERM that night, both rises were rescinded, one immediately and one the following day.

The political fallout

Economists often forget that exchange rate crises can be shattering experiences for those directly involved. The 1949 and 1967 devaluations were serious political blows for the Labour administrations involved. Thatcher and Lawson were bruised after their experience in January and February 1985. After the ERM crisis the Major administration never regained its political authority. Yet the economic impact of the enforced policy shift in 1992 was beneficial. Devaluation helped exporters and enabled the government to reduce interest rates much more quickly than it could have done inside the ERM. As we noted in Chapter 5, inflation also continued to fall, contradicting the predictions of most economists, who expected it to rise. None of this ultimately helped the government, which had given the impression that it was powerless to influence events and therefore unable to take the credit as economic prospects improved.

Floating

From September 1992, the pound was left to float. Both the Major government and its Labour successor tried to maintain a neutral policy on the exchange rate. The pound was left to find its own market value without interference from government. As part of the new policy to target inflation directly, interest rates were adjusted (by the Chancellor under Conservative rule and subsequently by the Bank of England when Labour took office) solely on the basis of what was needed to stick to the inflation target. Yet still both governments were under considerable pressure because of the level of the exchange rate under their stewardship. Sterling gradually recovered most of the value it lost against other European currencies at the time of its exit from the ERM and went to appreciate above its ERM level: for much of the period 1997–9 the pound was close to or above three German marks. This led to strong protests from many sectors of industry: business people and economists argued that jobs were lost because of the difficulty of maintaining export markets with an uncompetitive or overvalued exchange rate. Both governments largely ignored the complaints of the export sector. They stuck with their commitment to the pursuit of low inflation (although this did not prevent some Labour ministers publicly trying to put pressure on the Bank of England to ease its policy stance in the light of the strength of sterling in 1998–9).

Whose interest?

This highlights the dilemma which policy-makers face. Cutting interest rates to satisfy the demands of one sector of the economy would have risked fuelling inflationary pressures in other sectors which are not export-led or so dependent on the exchange rate and which continued to grow strongly during this period. Different sectors of the economy may have different needs. It is the task of the macroeconomic policy-maker to determine what is in the best interest of the economy as a whole.

Economic and Monetary Union

If national economies have difficulty in adjusting to a central economic policy, how much more difficult is it to determine policy for a group of economies widely divergent in their structure? That is the challenge which eleven European countries set for themselves when EMU, the plan to replace national currencies with the euro – the single European currency – was launched on 1 January 1999. Although the UK chose not to join the first wave of EMU countries, the government had nevertheless to develop a policy towards the euro. The UK's attitude to, and likely participation in, the single-currency project was discussed in Chapter 4. Here we focus on the exchange rate implications. These are, of course, complex.

After the creation of the euro, the ten currencies affected (Luxembourg has long had a currency union with Belgium) had rates which were irrevocably locked for the three-year transition period. In 2002 the national currencies will be phased out altogether when euro notes and coins are introduced. As far as the foreign exchange markets were concerned, and for most international trading purposes, however, the euro replaced those national currencies from day one.

In the UK, the debate about whether it should ever join EMU, and when, remained controversial. But a reminder of the impact which the euro would have on British exchange rate policy, whatever the outcome of that debate, came in the first few months of the euro's life. Contrary to the predictions of many observers, the euro declined in value against the dollar and against the pound. This made life even more uncomfortable for British exporters, both those selling their goods within the euro zone and those competing against euro zone companies in other parts of the world.

The euro weakened partly because the economies of Europe, especially Germany, the dominant economy of the euro area, were in a much weaker state at the start of EMU than had been anticipated. But there were also tensions between the new European Central Bank, which was responsible for managing the euro, and national governments. Essentially, the Bank was keen to establish a reputation for independence and to demonstrate to the financial markets that the euro would, like the German mark before it, be a hard currency, one not prone to depreciation, because it was the product of a low-inflation zone. Political leaders within the euro zone, however, had different priorities: they wanted to avoid recession in their countries and wanted lower European interest rates to help achieve this.

The pound's problems were a by-product of these tensions. This position was hardly a new one for sterling. But it was a reminder of how frustrating it can be for British policy-makers, who find themselves trying to respond to exchange rate fluctuations which have their origins outside the UK but which have a direct impact on sterling and the British economy.

The powerlessness of government

As we noted at the beginning of this chapter, the UK is among the most open economies in the world in terms of the proportion of GDP accounted for by trade and investment flows. This makes the economy particularly sensitive, both economically and politically, to exchange rate movements. We have seen that constructing an exchange rate policy is difficult because of the wide variation in interests within the UK: no policy will satisfy all interests, or even most of them. But the principal obstacle is a practical one. Far more than previously, all economies by the end of the twentieth century were exposed to the power of the international financial markets.

In 1969, a Briton travelling abroad could take no more than £50 worth of foreign currency out of the country; almost no one had credit cards. The government was therefore able to exercise very tight control on the flows of money across the exchanges. Government intervention in the foreign exchange markets was easier and had a greater (though not certain) chance of success than today because non-governmental flows could be controlled. In 1979 it was still necessary to take your passport to the bank when buying foreign currency, since there were limits on the amounts you could purchase, for both individuals and businesses. But in the autumn of that year, all British exchange controls were abolished by the Thatcher government, which was committed to the free movement of both goods and capital around the world. Most other governments in the industrial world eventually followed suit, as did an increasing number of developing countries. By 1999, estimates suggest that in the London market alone some $400 billion (about 1 per cent of world GDP) of currency trading took place *every day*.

Capital flows around the world are huge. Since exchange rate values at their most basic reflect relative demand for one currency compared with another, it follows that exchange rate values will fluctuate in line with flows. Capital flows can have many different purposes. They can be trade-related flows: money moving across the exchanges because an individual or company with assets in one company wants or needs to purchase (or sell) something denominated in another. They can be investment flows: individuals or companies do not want to buy something moveable but want to invest overseas – in a factory or other physical asset which will stay where it is, or simply to buy equity in overseas companies. Such flows may reflect a business opportunity – the decision to become involved in economic activity elsewhere. Or they could be flows simply reflecting someone's desire to switch from one financial asset to another. US Treasury bonds, for example (in effect, loan certificates issued by the US government which offer a fixed rate of interest) may offer a better return than, say, Japanese government debt: people looking for a high return and not unduly worried about inflation differentials may switch their investment accordingly. If enough people were to do that, the US dollar would rise and the yen fall. Such flows are sometimes called 'hot money' – financial flows not linked to physical economic activity but simply chasing the best return.

It is these last which make national economies most vulnerable to exchange rate fluctuations mainly because of the scale of these capital movements. A herd instinct seems to operate in financial markets: traders may not be sure about the relative merits of one currency against another, but if sufficient funds start to flow out of one currency most traders will follow the general pattern. All these trends became more pronounced as electronic technology hugely increased the speed of transactions. As trading activity rose, many financial institutions which had previously executed transactions only on behalf of their clients began to trade on a large scale in their own right – what is known as proprietary trading.

Controlling the markets

During the last decade of the century another development in international financial trading added to the difficulties of exchange rate policy-making, and created new problems relating to financial supervision. This was the rapid growth of sophisticated instruments which enabled investors and traders to speculate about the future movements of exchange rates. *Hedging* is essentially a form of insurance, designed for people and businesses who are committed to making or receiving a payment in a foreign currency at a specific point in the future. In exchange for a premium, a financial institution will guarantee the rate for a certain date. An alternative is the *forward* foreign currency market: someone holding pounds, for example, can buy another currency, such as dollars, in this market – this is a binding commitment to exchange the currency at a specified rate and time in the future. Or, if you are not sure you will want or need to buy another currency, you can buy *options*. These give you the option to exchange at a predetermined rate, but there is no obligation to take up the option if you choose not to: perhaps because currency movements have shifted in an unexpected direction or perhaps because you no longer need the other currency. Of course, all these instruments carry a fee.

As foreign exchange markets grew exponentially, and electronic trading made more and more sophisticated transactions possible, the number and complexity of these financial *derivatives*, as they are termed, soared. These instruments are no longer devices to enable the business person to trade abroad with less risk. They are often solely designed to maximise the return on money – by switching it around the world at high speed and by constructing both complex devices that often depend on correctly predicting exchange rate movements and equally complex devices to try to ensure against getting such predictions wrong.

The danger with many of these derivatives is their opacity. Because very little money is transferred until the deal is concluded, which is often some months or even years away from the time of the initial transaction, very large gambles can be made with relatively few resources. A small down payment can disguise the extent of the potential commitment and thus the risk if anything goes wrong. The exposure involved is therefore highly *leveraged*. Getting predictions right can make profits of hundreds of millions of dollars for the hedge funds which specialise in this; getting it wrong can bring large institutions to the point of collapse. In the late 1990s there were several spectacular examples of this happening. In 1995, Barings Bank in London collapsed because of the activities of one of its traders in Singapore. In 1998 an American fund, LTCM, had to be rescued by a consortium of international banks, which were persuaded to do so by the American authorities, worried about market panic. It subsequently transpired that some British banks had significant exposure to this fund in the event of its collapse.

The supervisory issues which such activities raise are therefore substantial. How can one government, or, indeed, several, ensure that such trading is properly executed, that financial institutions do not place themselves and their depositors' money at too great a risk? How can capital flows, which have both domestic and international policy implications, be regulated? The answer is with extreme difficulty, because there will always be somewhere that financial institutions can base themselves to escape what they regard as too much scrutiny. Authorities around the world have found it increasingly difficult to tackle these issues as technological advances make actual geographical location less and less important for those involved in moving money across the exchanges and around the world.

All these activities have implications for exchange rate policy, since many of them depend on movements in exchange rates in one direction or the other. The prospect of large profits to be had in the event of currency movements in a particular direction can increase speculative activity. Once it becomes clear that a currency is moving in a certain direction, there is an even greater incentive for everyone in the market to follow suit, to minimise their exposure to risk. The days leading up to sterling's enforced departure from the ERM in 1992 and the subsequent devaluation provided British policy-makers with a powerful sense of this. Until trading within the ERM ceased at 4 p.m. on 16 September, the Bank of England was obliged to exchange pounds for those wanting to sell them at the prevailing ERM rate (about DM2.73), yet the day after those pounds would be worth only something like DM2.50. The cost to the British authorities of this exercise was huge. The scale of the gains of those speculators who switched their funds in time were equally large. It was an object lesson in the risks governments face when adopting a fixed exchange rate in a world of free capital movements. Abandoning commitments with such a high potential price tag is therefore attractive. But as this chapter has sought to show, letting the pound move where the markets choose does not let policy-makers off the hook. Whatever they may say in public, governments always have a view about where they would like the exchange rate to be. That view may be difficult to arrive at, but it will inevitably affect what they do.

9 Public spending

What is public spending for?

The underlying rationale for public spending is clear: it is for the provision of public goods. These, broadly, are goods from which society as a whole benefits but which either will not benefit individuals sufficiently to persuade them to make provision themselves, or can be provided more cheaply on a collective than on an individual basis. For the early economic theorists, such as the eighteenth-century Scottish economist Adam Smith, public goods were extremely limited: military defence of the nation was the paramount example. This view has modified over the centuries as successive British governments became increasingly involved in the life of the individual. By the early years of the twentieth century, government – at both national and local level – had assumed some responsibility for education, pensions and national insurance and housing.

The Second World War radically altered both the levels of public spending and attitudes to it. Government spending had soared during the six years of war. This had a sort of ratchet effect – it is always easier to increase than cut spending. At the same time, the 1942 Beveridge report on social insurance, the 1944 White Paper *Employment Policy* and the Education Act of the same year, the incoming Labour government's commitment to a publicly funded national health service, all marked a clear shift in the accepted view of the role of government in the provision of goods and services.

It became accepted, right across the political spectrum, that government had a responsibility to provide services like education and health, and that, moreover, the state could provide them more cheaply. It was seen to be in the interests of society as a whole that individuals were healthier and better educated. In the longer term, more people would be able to remain independent and not forced to rely on some kind of

171

welfare benefit, but the economy as a whole would benefit from more output, produced more efficiently.

The Labour government which came to office in 1945 also took the view that some sectors of economic activity should be directly controlled by the state: it moved swiftly to nationalise public utilities, the railway system and the iron and steel industry. Here the underlying motivation and rationale was more complex. In part, at least, the argument was one of efficiency: a single national railway system, for

Table 9.1 The growth of public spending

Year	£billion at 1990 prices	Year	£billion at 1990 prices
1948	51.84	1973	89.19
1949	54.77	1974	90.80
1950	54.64	1975	95.75
1951	58.69	1976	97.00
1952	64.48	1977	95.36
1953	66.16	1978	97.44
1954	65.88	1979	99.28
1955	64.15	1980	101.01
1956	63.49	1981	101.26
1957	62.43	1982	102.15
1958	60.77	1983	104.30
1959	61.83	1984	105.18
1960	63.05	1985	105.10
1961	65.27	1986	106.82
1962	67.27	1987	107.86
1963	69.41	1988	108.61
1964	70.63	1989	110.14
1965	72.67	1990	112.93
1966	74.76	1991	115.85
1967	78.96	1992	115.73
1968	79.36	1993	115.52
1969	77.99	1994	118.08
1970	79.37	1995	119.58
1971	81.79	1996	121.05
1972	85.40	1997	121.34

The table illustrates the growth of public spending since 1948: the figures are for general government expenditure at constant 1990 prices.
Data from the Office for National Statistics.

instance, would make more sense than the existing series of competing companies. But Labour's philosophy of nationalisation also owed much to the belief that the workers themselves, with the state acting as proxy, ought to own key areas of economic output such as iron and steel.

The consequence of these attitudinal changes was a sharp rise in public spending after 1945 (see Table 9.1). This increased spending had to be financed – the government had to raise the money for it, either through increased taxation or through borrowing, or through a combination of both. This had consequences for fiscal policy (see Chapter 7). It also had consequences for the planning and management of spending: huge sums of money went on a large range of programmes which touched on almost every aspect of economic life.

How the spending system works

Every pound the government spends has to be approved by Parliament. All spending plans are therefore submitted in the 'Estimates' which the government of the day sends to Parliament. The main Estimates go once a year; any additional funds needed must be approved in 'Supplementary Estimates'. The Treasury official responsible for this is known as the Estimates Clerk. Spending is divided into categories closely linked to the government department which is ultimately responsible for disbursing the funds approved.

But Parliamentary control, while still seen as important, does not have much to do with the way the government of the day manages the spending total, nor with the way spending resources are allocated among government departments. This is also done by the Treasury, which, after 1979, controlled spending on a three-year rolling programme. The current system is based, somewhat loosely, on the arrangements put in place following the Plowden report in 1961. Before the 1960s, there was no formal system for planning spending – everything was done on a more *ad hoc* basis. Plowden recommended a system of resource-based planning to enable the government to take strategic decisions about the total amount it should spend, and within that total to allocate resources according to an agreed set of priorities. In the years immediately after its establishment, this system was widely admired and many other countries sought to follow its example.

Since Plowden, there has been an annual cycle for public spending, although from 1997 this has been significantly modified (see below).

The key ministers are the Chancellor and his second in command at the Treasury, the Chief Secretary, who is specifically responsible for spending matters. Essentially, the Treasury would fix the total amount of spending for any one year, and indicate its provisional plans for the following two years. These figures would then be approved by the whole Cabinet, usually in July. Spending departments and their ministers could try bidding for more money than the Treasury's plans allowed for. But the burden would be on them to argue their case strongly, since their gain would be another department's loss. Overall annual figures are still decided by the Treasury and subject to some modification each year. But the centrepiece of the new system is the three-yearly Comprehensive Spending Review, which seeks to fix allocations for three years ahead, with no intermediate review, thus limiting the opportunity for spending ministers to argue the case for additional funds.

One of the weaknesses of the system put in place following the Plowden report had originally been seen as one of its strengths. It was resource based: departments knew how much money in real terms (i.e. after allowing for the effects of inflation) they were going to get for several years ahead. But when inflation took off in the 1970s, the government's spending bill soared. This made it difficult for government to keep a grip on the spending total and it added to inflationary pressures in the economy. In 1975, cash limits were introduced. These capped spending in cash terms: spending programmes no longer automatically rose in line with inflation. In 1981–2, the planning system also switched to a cash basis. Departments were given allocations on the basis of an inflation assumption, and their allocations were no longer automatically adjusted if that assumption turned out to be wrong. A separate decision would then be taken about providing money from the Contingency Reserve – the pocket of spending which the Chancellor keeps unallocated.

The extent of Treasury control

Other refinements during the 1980s and 1990s were aimed at strengthening the Treasury's control over the spending process. Ensuring that the Cabinet as a whole signed up to the Chancellor's total was the first step. The consequences of this were that departmental ministers knew that they would be, in effect, fighting with each other rather than the

Chancellor and Chief Secretary for any increased resources. Until the 1980s, the Chief Secretary conducted separate bilateral negotiations with each minister; this meant that any increases in one department's spending programme would oblige the Chief Secretary to find off-setting savings elsewhere. The Treasury was the initial arbiter of disagreements, and unresolved disputes went to a small committee of ministers chaired by a senior and neutral minister (this was known informally as the Star Chamber) to be sorted out. This approach diluted the Treasury's influence. With the revised arrangements intro-duced by the Major government, the overall spending total came to represent a zero-sum game, to be resolved by individual ministers themselves.

Individual spending ministers are unlikely to have very clear views about the public expenditure total. They do not have access to the Treasury's internal deliberations about the macro-picture; nor do their officials. It is difficult for any minister, other than the Prime Minister (who will already have discussed the issues privately), to take issue with the Chancellor's plans. But the Chancellor and his Treasury colleagues and officials will have very clear views about the competing claims of spending ministers. The Treasury view on where increased spending should go, or where planned cuts should be imposed, will very often prevail.

In part, this will reflect the fact that from a macroeconomic policy viewpoint not all spending is equal. Increasing resources devoted to unemployment and job creation will seem more attractive at a time of rising unemployment, for example, than, say, more spending on the arts. Equally, the Chancellor and his officials will be wary of imposing cuts on politically sensitive areas such as NHS expenditure. Individual ministers may seek to take credit for increases in spending in their areas; the Chancellor is likely to be blamed for cuts.

It is important to note, in this context and more generally, the misleading use of terminology employed when talking about increases and cuts in spending. It is rare for spending on individual programmes to be cut in absolute terms. When critics or disappointed ministers speak of cuts they nearly always mean cuts in *previously planned spending increases*. The only major area of spending to see substantial real cuts in recent years has been the defence programme. This re-flected a widely accepted view that the end of the Cold War provided an opportunity to make significant reductions in Britain's defence commitments.

The Comprehensive Spending Review

The election of the Labour government in 1997 brought further changes. Chancellor Gordon Brown introduced a Comprehensive Spending Review, intended to take place every third year. The Review is meant to examine all areas of public spending in a much more radical way than hitherto, with each department having to justify its spending total; in this way, the Treasury gets the opportunity to look afresh at the government's spending priorities and the room for manoeuvre. In the years between each Review, however, the intention is to limit changes to the previously announced plans and thus to move away from the annual cycle. The Review is intended to give departments the chance to look at their internal allocation of spending priorities and to improve inter-departmental co-ordination of spending where several departments are involved. But it is likely to tighten the Treasury's control still further, since it alone can take the overview of government spending needed to make the Review effective. And each three-yearly allocation of resources to departments involves a commitment from them to meet efficiency savings.

Changing attitudes to spending

The Thatcher government came to power in 1979 committed to a substantial overhaul of public spending. Margaret Thatcher wanted to re-open the question of what the government should spend money on; she also wanted to reduce both the spending total and the share of GDP accounted for by public spending. On both counts it could be argued that she ultimately failed. Absolute spending in real terms rose inexorably (see Table 9.1). It is true that spending as a percentage of GDP fell slightly during Thatcher's premiership. But the recession induced by her government's struggle to curb the inflationary surge of the late 1980s (see Chapter 5) meant that within three years of her leaving office it was back almost to the level of 1979–80. By the 1990s, however, both the Conservative and Labour parties were committed to cutting this figure and after several years of sustained economic growth, combined with more effective control of the spending total, the spending ratio did begin to fall. The total continued to rise, but it did so at a lower rate than output (GDP).

Thatcher successfully re-opened the debate about what government should spend money on. Some areas of spending activity had been eliminated during the 1980s. Few policy-makers now argue seriously for large-scale state aid to industry, for instance: they may argue the case for some spending to attract new foreign direct investment, but they will not seek to justify the rescue of companies about to collapse. In the 1990s this debate become far more radical. For most of the post-war period, welfare spending had been seen by successive governments as untouchable. But as the social security bill soared so too did the social problems which welfare spending was at least in part intended to alleviate. The number of people living in poverty grew; Britain had the highest rate of teenage pregnancies in Europe; and the number of people who were unemployed for more than a year remained stubbornly high. With the very high levels of unemployment in the early 1980s it was not surprising that the cost of unemployment benefit and associated social programmes rose sharply. But when unemployment fell, welfare spending did not fall with it. Policy-makers grew alarmed in the 1990s as size of the social security bill, and the share of national income which it accounted for, grew to levels not anticipated even thirty years earlier.

Tackling welfare

Both John Major and his successor, Tony Blair, recognised the need to bring the social security bill under control. But this proved politically and practically difficult. Both governments made great efforts to cut fraudulent social security claims. Policy-makers recognised that in some centrally funded welfare programmes and in programmes run by local authorities, such as housing benefit, there was substantial scope for, and occurrence of, fraud. Money invested in extra effort to detect fraud tended to bring substantial returns. But this was a sensitive area: ministers did not want to be seen to be attempting to deprive people of their legitimate entitlement. Moreover, in the final analysis, while eliminating all or at least reducing fraud can bring useful savings, it was clear that this was not the heart of the problem of the burgeoning bill.

This remains a major problem for policy-makers, and is clearly not one easily solved. Moreover, it touches on one of the most sensitive issues relating to social welfare payments – means-testing. That is, claimants have to demonstrate their individual need for help by providing detailed information about their income, savings and number of dependants: only if they meet the eligibility criteria for the benefit will they receive it. The vast and complex array of social spending programmes developed in a haphazard way as successive governments tried both to tackle poverty and to enhance the safety net for those in need. Some benefits are payable irrespective of an individual's economic circumstance. Child benefit – a payment made to parents for each child – is an example of this. Someone earning, say, £100,000 a year gets the same amount of benefit per child as someone who is unemployed. Other benefits are means-tested.

Means-testing has always been politically controversial. Some argue that it makes no sense to pay wealthy people an indiscriminate social benefit, and want to see means-testing on all forms of welfare payment. Others are opposed to means-testing in principle, in part because they believe it can dissuade genuinely needy people from making a claim. With the very sharp rise in social security spending in the 1990s, however, means-testing came to be seen by many policy-makers as inevitable.

Transfer payments

The black hole of welfare spending highlights a major division in public spending which is often overlooked. Government spending can be divided into two principal categories: the provision of goods and services for consumption; and government transfers, that is the transfer of money from one section of the population to another via the government tax and benefit system. Reforms in public spending have vastly improved the government's ability to control its spending on goods and services. Voters may complain about the level of provision of education, health or defence, for example: but the government is much more successful than it used to be at achieving the spending target it sets for itself. These programmes have, in general, been brought under tight control, with growth being at a pace predetermined by the Treasury.

But government transfers account for more than half of all public spending, and they are far more difficult to control effectively. Some transfers involve the government collecting money (in the form of taxes) from all taxpayers and redistributing this money to another group, which includes all or some of those taxpayers. Child benefit is an example of this: anyone with a child is eligible for child benefit, so some taxpayers (though not those without children) will, in effect, get their tax contribution back. A redistribution clearly takes place, but not one based on relative wealth.

Other transfers do involve a specific redistribution of income and wealth from the rich (taxpayers) to the poor (non-taxpayers). The challenge facing policy-makers is to determine whether these transfers redistribute in a sensible and fair way, and one which can be controlled. The need for control is likely to become more pressing because of demographic factors now at work. Already one of the biggest areas of welfare spending is on provision for the elderly. The number of elderly people is growing rapidly both in absolute terms and as a proportion of the population: medical technology has improved life expectancy and birth rates have dropped. The state pension bill will obviously rise in line with the number of pensioners. But health care costs will also rise: elderly people are more likely to need medical care, including hospital provision, than younger members of the population. A growing elderly population is also likely to make great demands on other services, such as domestic social services provision. These demographic changes are likely to place considerable pressure on public spending.

This, though, is only one consequence of the demographic changes already taking place (not just in Britain but in all industrial countries). The other is a projected decline in the number of people of working age. At a time when demands on public services and pension provision will be rising, the proportion of the population able to finance such provision will be falling. For economic policy-makers this represents a particularly difficult challenge. We have seen in earlier chapters that much economic policy is inevitably of a short-term nature: a matter of balancing different, often contradictory objectives – inflation and un-employment, spending and taxation. Policy cannot be made in a vacuum. It has to respond to developments in the real world, sometimes outside the UK, frequently beyond the influence of policy-makers. Long-term planning is difficult, overtaken as it often is by events which are usually unexpected. But the policy implications of these demographic changes cannot be ignored, since the changes threaten the fragile consensus which exists about the provision of, and funding for, public services and pensions.

The pressure on resources

Rising demand for health care provision, for example, should not be underestimated, since the growing number of elderly people dependent on the NHS coincides with developments in medical science which will also lead to greater demands being placed on it. The more doctors can cure, or at least treat, previously incurable illnesses, such as some forms of cancer or heart disease, the more money will be needed to provide such treatments. From its inception, the NHS has, in practice, relied on various forms of rationing to operate within the funding limits set by government. Periodically (usually close to general elections) there are bouts of hysteria about waiting lists for operations, or the rationing of kidney dialysis treatment, for example. Those encouraging such outbursts usually have an ulterior political motive. No politician, however, has ever been willing to admit what some policy-makers will concede in private: that medical science is already so far advanced that the UK could double or treble spending on health care and still not have the resources to tackle every treatable illness. In practice, any such public service must operate some form of rationing, which ultimately involves putting a price on human life. In economic terms, the judgement to be made is essentially one which calculates the marginal cost of saving a life, and at some point that marginal cost will be judged to be greater than society as a whole is willing to pay.

These are hugely difficult and sensitive decisions and they tend to be fudged because of a general reluctance to discuss them explicitly. But the pressure to be more transparent about these issues is likely to grow as medical technology advances. Should doctors, for example, be free to prescribe treatments whatever the cost, even if there is only a very small chance of extending a patient's life? Such questions become far more difficult when the patient is perhaps eighty or ninety years old. While these issues undoubtedly have a moral and social dimension they are, fundamentally, economic, both in the sense that a state can ultimately spend only the resources it has; and that the state, or those acting on its behalf, must make decisions about the competing demands on those resources. Moral and practical difficulties of this kind led Adam Smith and his intellectual successors to take the view that the individual is usually best placed to make such judgements in his or her interest.

Pensions

Pension payments are another potential source of controversy. Since the amount payable for each pensioner is fixed, the amount payable by the Exchequer in any one year will depend on the number of pensioners.

Those payments come from the taxes collected from those still in work. There is an implicit inter-generational bargain involved. Those people who are now pensioners contributed, as workers and taxpayers, to the pensions of their parents and grandparents on the understanding that their pensions would be paid for by the generation now in work. But as people live longer and the number of pensioners grows, this bargain is under threat. If too few taxpayers were expected to fund a growing number of pensioners, resistance to the higher taxes which might be needed would grow. This is not to suggest that future generations will necessarily be more hard-hearted or selfish, but simply that, as we saw with the potential difficulties with heath care provision, the choices facing a state with increased competition for (relatively) scarce resources may become much more difficult.

Since the 1980s, successive governments have recognised the need to respond to this problem, although their attempts to tackle it have met with mixed success. The most radical change was introduced in 1981 by the Thatcher government, though few recognised its full significance at the time. It changed the way the basic old-age pension was calculated. Until that point, pensions had been up-rated in line with the annual increase in earnings, but this was changed so that pensions were subsequently linked to the rate of inflation. This indexation protects pensioners from the erosion of their income by high inflation. But because average earnings have risen significantly faster than inflation, the old-age pension has fallen relative to average incomes, from its peak of 20 per cent in 1977 to 15 per cent in 1999; it is projected to fall to around 7.5 per cent by 2050. Many more pensioners now rely on additional welfare payments, such as income support. As the full significance and consequence of the up-rating change were recognised, pressure grew for it to be reversed. These were resisted. However unpalatable the change, it meant the UK had taken the first steps towards tackling the much bigger problem of pension reform.

The Thatcher administration also actively encouraged people to make their own private pension provision. Policy-makers realised that one way of shifting the pension burden away from the state before it became unsustainable would be for individuals to make their own arrangements to supplement their basic pension. For many years some employers, including the civil service, had provided occupational pension schemes, usually involving contributions from both employer and employee. The pension payable on retirement was then linked to the individual's salary.

In the mid-1970s, the Labour government had introduced a state version of this for those without occupational pension schemes: the State Earnings Related Pension Scheme (SERPS) was a second pension related to an individual's earnings and compulsory for those who did not belong to an occupational scheme. But it had become clear by the late 1980s that SERPS, although contribution-based, was likely to make the longer-term problem of state pensions worse because of the mounting liabilities of the scheme. Arrangements were introduced, therefore, to encourage everyone to make private provision for their pension. Tax incentives were greatly enhanced for those seeking to pay contributions into a private scheme, and those in occupational schemes had the option of setting up their own pension arrangements if they preferred, and so too could those in SERPS.

These plans suffered a major setback when it was discovered that the private pensions industry had been guilty of giving poor advice to many people looking to set up their own arrangements. It transpired that huge numbers of people had been the victim of pensions 'misselling' – they had wrongly been encouraged by salespeople to leave occupational schemes or SERPS, leaving them potentially worse off than before. The effort to sort the mess out, and compensate those who were the victims of poor or dishonest advice, took several years, and brought the entire industry into disrepute.

It did not, however, change the views of policy-makers who argued that the only long-term solution was to make individuals themselves responsible for a much larger proportion of their post-retirement income. The Labour government which took office in 1997 was committed to this approach. It announced plans to introduce a two-tier pension scheme: everyone will get the state pension but be obliged to take out a second pension. For those on low incomes and who have neither an occupational nor a normal private pension, this will be provided for by the private sector but operated under government guidelines.

Current versus capital spending

Planning for the long term is difficult for policy-makers, partly for the logistical reasons mentioned above, but also because the political process is heavily biased towards the short term. Policy-makers may spend time and effort trying to assess and resolve future problems but politicians tend, on the whole, to have five-year time horizons at most, in line with the cycle of general elections. Public spending is an area where the long term and the short term often conflict. If ministers approve a rise in spending, they would prefer to see it bear fruit sooner rather than later: more nurses and teachers are more visible than hospital or school building commitments. Equally, if reductions in planned spending are imposed, it is easier to cancel a new school not yet built. But this approach to public spending, which prevailed until the mid-1990s, completely blurs the distinction between current and capital spending. Current spending includes all spending which may be classed as recurring or routine – salaries, running costs, heating and lighting of public buildings and so on; capital means investment in buildings and equipment. This distinction is one familiar to private companies and accountants, but it was not much heeded when considering overall levels of public spending.

The failure to distinguish between the two types of spending had important consequences. Consider the example of education. During the mid-1970s, when planned expenditure was being cut back because of economic difficulties, it was much easier for the old Department of Education and Science to postpone the building of new schools to replace ageing Victorian buildings. The Treasury was interested solely in total figures – departments and their ministers were left to come up with savings as they saw fit. But postponing or cutting an item of capital expenditure can actually lead to a rise in current spending in future years. An old school will need more money spent on repairs than a new one; it will be less efficient and therefore more expensive to heat. The saving offered, then, is only a saving in the short term and shifts more expenditure into the future. The old building will at some point have to be replaced and in the meantime current spending will be higher than it otherwise would have been.

In the 1990s, the Major government sought to make the distinction between current and capital spending clearer. But Gordon Brown went much further, reintroducing the so-called 'golden rule' which separated the two types of spending in the national accounts and prohibited government borrowing to fund current spending (see Chapter 7).

The Private Finance Initiative

Another and more controversial innovation which dates from the 1980s is the Private Finance Initiative (PFI). This was initially conceived as a way of making sure some important capital projects went ahead in spite of tight public spending restrictions. The idea was to bring some private sector capital into projects that would normally be wholly the responsibility of the public sector. Roads, hospitals and other construction projects were regarded as suitable. So a plan to build an extra motorway in the heavily congested area around Birmingham was put out for tender by private contractors. Instead of being paid a fee by the government to build the road, the contractors were expected to put up the money themselves, in return for which they would retain management of the road and be permitted to charge a toll for drivers wishing to use it. When completed, the UK's road system will have been improved but the government will not have had to spend or borrow money to achieve this.

The PFI attracted bipartisan support, in part because the prospect of increasing provision of public capital projects without increasing total public spending is irresistible to politicians. Some economists and government officials were sceptical of the benefits. Their arguments usually centred on the issue of risk: who was ultimately liable if a project ran into difficulties? The sceptics argued that the government was, and that therefore such projects properly belonged in the public rather than the private sector. In the event, PFI projects have been limited in number for practical reasons – principally the complexity of the negotiations involved.

Local spending

Most public spending is determined centrally, but significant amounts are actually spent by local government. Local authorities have substantial budgets of their own, and spend money on a range of services from street cleaning to social services. Much education spending is handled at the local level, as are housing benefit payments. The arrangements for local spending are among the most complex of any of the spending programmes. This is for two main reasons: first, the extent to which local authorities are forced to rely on central government grants for their revenue (see Chapter 7); and second, because central government in practice directs much of what local government spends money on. Housing benefit payments – supplements paid to people in rented accommodation towards their housing costs – are administered locally but determined nationally: local government acts as the agent for central government.

Much of the rest of local government spending is also determined nationally, at least in part. Local authorities have statutory responsibilities in relation to some basic provisions such as street cleaning. They also have only very limited freedom within large areas of the budget: education, the largest single item in any local council budget, is primarily the disbursement of money according to the rules set out by the Department for Education and Employment.

Local authorities have found their freedom to undertake discretionary spending increasingly restricted because of the shortage of funds at their disposal and because of central government's desire to control the overall public spending total. They faced even tougher controls on what they could do after 1981–2, when rate-capping was introduced. This was a mechanism which limited local authorities' ability to raise money from local sources – rates (property taxes), subsequently replaced by the community charge or poll tax in 1990 (1989 in Scotland) and the council tax (another property tax) in 1993 (see Box 7.2, page 150).

Public spending has therefore become more centralised within the UK. National policy-makers probably now have more control over all aspects of public spending – both the amounts and what it is spent on – than at any time previously. Much of that national control lies within the Treasury, which has consolidated its power in this area, a move which, for different political reasons, has been overseen by governments of both main political parties.

Devolution

In 1999, a new tier of spending authority was introduced into some parts of the UK when the Labour government's promises on devolution came to fruition. The new Scottish Parliament acquired two important powers: one was the ability to determine how to spend a good proportion of the funds allocated to Scotland; the other was a very limited revenue-raising power. In Wales, the new Assembly did not get revenue-raising powers, but it too acquired discretion over important parts of government spending in Wales. In late 1999, as part of the peace process, Northern Ireland, too, acquired a devolved administration. The new administrations can have only a small effect on total public spending in the UK. But they could alter the pattern of spending in parts of the UK, although it will be several years before the impact of these changes can be assessed.

Accountability

But who checks the Treasury? In one sense, no one, since its political masters are accountable to Parliament and, ultimately, to voters at election times. But there is, in fact, an elaborate series of arrangements for ensuring that money is spent properly and for the purposes it is designed for. The Comptroller and Auditor General is an official accountable directly to Parliament, who – through the National Audit Office – audits the government's books, ensuring that government departments spend money properly. The National Audit Office has responsibilities for a wide range of public spending, by local authorities and government agencies. The Public Accounts Committee of the House of Commons has considerable power to examine those with responsibility for government spending. It can censure individuals or departments charged with wrongdoing. The Audit Commission monitors spending by local government in the same way.

The Permanent Secretary (the most senior official) of each government department is that department's accounting officer: he or she is personally responsible for all the spending controlled by the department and, consequently, for any misuse of funds. In the UK, the custom is that officials advise, ministers decide, and ministers take final responsibility for their actions. The Accounting Officer role of the Permanent Secretary is the exception to this and is therefore taken extremely seriously by those concerned.

10 Industrial policy and economic growth

What is industrial policy?

Most governments would say that their long-term aim is to increase prosperity for the national economy. That this is usually an explicit objective is, arguably, a post-war phenomenon, but not exclusively so. The active encouragement of the Industrial Revolution in the eighteenth century and of further innovation in the nineteenth was an indication of the importance policy-makers even then placed on national prosperity, and the link between prosperity and industry was firmly established. Nor are government concerns about British industrial performance particularly new. The Royal Commission on Technical Instruction which reported in 1882 catalogued the weaknesses of British industry and management. Its list of indictments would make familiar reading today: not enough proper training for workers; insufficient emphasis placed on technical as opposed to managerial skills; poor linguistic attainment compared with foreign competitors. Others have been added more recently: a failure on the part of industry to invest; a failure of financiers, especially those based in the City of London, to invest in domestic industry; too great an emphasis on the need for short-term returns.

But though they may be worried about British industry's record, should governments do anything about it? Should government actively seek to promote rising prosperity and rising individual living standards? And should it do so by pursuing an industrial policy which ensures British industry will be competitive on world markets and at home?

These are not rhetorical questions. They go to the heart of the debate about what economic policy is for and what it should comprise. They also touch on one of the most controversial aspects of economic policy in the post-war period: whether there should be a national industrial policy, and what it should be. For much of the twentieth century it was one of the issues which most clearly divided the two main political parties; it was also the issue which revealed the widest gap between what governments said and what they did.

In earlier chapters we have noted the extensive interaction between different aspects of economic life, the difficulty of establishing cause and effect. This is just as true of industrial policy. In practice, all governments have an industrial policy. Deciding to do nothing is not actually an option, whatever the free-marketeers may say. Changes in taxation of individuals and companies; counter-inflationary policy; the exchange rate; membership of the EU: all have far-reaching implications for the way companies conduct their affairs. Since the Second World War, there have also been four areas of policy which have been directly concerned with industrial activity.

Nationalisation

The first of these was the long-running debate about nationalisation. British governments had a long tradition of such geopolitical links with industry. In 1914, for instance, the government had acquired a 51 per cent stake in what was then the Anglo-Persian Oil Company, which became the Anglo-Iranian Oil Company and which was renamed British Petroleum in 1954. There were also isolated examples of nationalisation. In 1931, the London transport system was taken into public ownership, as the London Passenger Transport Board.

In 1945, however, the Labour government came to power committed to a large-scale programme of nationalisation. This was a longstanding commitment and had its ideological roots in the days of the party's formation as the political wing of the trade union movement. Labour advocated shared ownership of the 'commanding heights of the economy', believing that the workers should share in the ownership of the most important areas of economic activity: power generation; food supply; the iron and steel and shipbuilding industries; and transport. In spite of the scale of economic problems which the new government inherited, it moved swiftly to implement its commitment on nationalisation.

Some of these state take-overs were seen as sensible on grounds of efficiency, particularly in the case of the nationalisation of the rail system and the main public utilities, as many of the pre-war owners had acquired a reputation for inefficient management. But others, especially the nationalisation of the iron and steel industry, divided people on ideological grounds. That industry was denationalised by the Conservatives in 1953 and renationalised by Labour in 1967.

Many of the nationalised industries failed to deliver. They acquired dismal records for poor customer service, industrial unrest and inefficient operation. They became increasingly unpopular among both policy-makers and citizens. The blame for these failings cannot be laid entirely at the door of the management of these industries. They were given little freedom of manoeuvre, and were subject to tight control and interference from ministers and officials, who often became involved in the day-to-day running of these industries. The Treasury controlled the level of subsidies which some industries received. It also determined how much they could invest – even if they were in surplus. Investment levels were not determined by the needs of the industry but by the needs of fiscal policy. For somewhat complicated historical reasons, nationalised industry investment levels counted as part of the total public sector borrowing requirement, and were thus subservient to the government's policy on this. The weaknesses of this approach were increasingly recognised by policy-makers at both official and political level, but the problems were not resolved until the Thatcher government launched its strategy of privatisation in the 1980s (see below).

Picking winners

By the time Labour regained office in the 1960s, it had developed a new and in some respects more interventionist approach to industrial policy. The new government was keenly aware of the poor record of British industry since the war. Ministers wanted to ensure Britain did not fall further behind its industrialised neighbours. The government was committed to giving a much greater strategic direction to the economy, achieving planned levels of output and raising the annual growth capacity of the economy by means of the National Plan, published in 1965 (see Chapter 2). The Plan, by its very nature, implied a considerable degree of direction over the activity of private industry. More generally, ministers wanted to encourage co-operation, domestically and internationally, between individual companies where they felt this was appropriate (what they called 'selective intervention') and on occasion to encourage strategic mergers to ensure that British industry was more able to compete effectively. The Industrial Re-organisation Corporation was set up to facilitate this: the creation of British Leyland in 1968, following a series of take-overs and mergers within the fragmented British car industry, was an example of this attempt to strengthen British industry.

Tony Benn, Minister of Technology from 1966 to 1970, was a prime exponent of this interventionist approach. When Labour returned to power in 1974, Benn became Industry Secretary. He oversaw the creation of the National Enterprise Board (NEB), a body charged with selecting and supporting the areas of industry in which Britain could compete effectively in the international economy. The NEB's job, therefore, was to 'pick winners', and it had investment funds to help fill the gap resulting from the alleged shortage of industrial investment funds in Britain. It was killed off by the Thatcher government, which was ideologically opposed to such active government intervention in industry.

Lame ducks

It became the accepted wisdom in the 1980s and 1990s that market forces should be left to operate freely, as this was the best way to ensure the survival of a strong British industrial sector. But even the most committed of free market governments have found this a difficult philosophy to pursue in practice. From the 1960s onwards, Britain's decaying industrial base presented ministers of both parties and of all ideological persuasions with a series of what were at least political, if not always economic, crises. Business was, by and large, heavily critical of any attempt by government to interfere in the way it conducted its affairs. But as policy-makers came to realise, indust-rialists took a different view when they got into financial trouble: then they were keen to have government help.

When the Heath government came to power in 1970, it was ex-plicitly committed to disengagement from the economy. Government, in Edward Heath's view, had no place in trying to run business. But barely a year later, the government found itself faced with the impend-ing collapse of Rolls-Royce, one of the world's leading makers of aero-engines and one of Britain's most high-profile companies. The choice presented to policy-makers was stark: refuse to help, and preside over the politically sensitive loss of thousands of jobs and of Britain's continuing role in a key sector of global industry; or pour large sums of money into the company. After much wrangling, the decision was taken to nationalise Rolls-Royce and inject substantial public capital into it. This was not what the company had wanted, and certainly not what the government had desired, but no satisfactory alternative was seen with such large amounts of taxpayers' money involved. The commitment to unfettered private enterprise had been ditched.

In the 1970s, both the Conservative and Labour governments found themselves trying to rescue one lame duck company after another. The car industry had more lame ducks than most. In 1975 the Labour government had to put huge sums into Chrysler, to prevent the American-owned carmaker closing down its British operation with the loss of thousands of jobs. And efforts to rescue the only British-owned car-maker dogged successive British governments from the 1970s until the end of the century. British Leyland, as it then was, was nationalised in 1975 to save it from collapse. Hundreds of millions of pounds of taxpayers' money subsequently went into the company, which had been dogged by poor industrial relations and a reputation for badly made cars. The Thatcher government, adamantly opposed to any kind of state aid for lame duck industries, found itself providing the company with nearly £700 million in state aid simply to try to ready the company for privatisation. Long after the company had moved back into the private sector, bought by British Aerospace, and by then known as the Rover Group, it continued to cause trouble. It was sold in 1995 to the German carmaker BMW but, in 1999, the Blair government ended up providing £150 million worth of grants to prevent BMW switching most Rover production outside the UK.

Why would governments so philosophically opposed to the idea of state intervention go to such lengths – and expense – to do the opposite of what they said they wanted? Part of the answer is about political reality: many of the decisions made by government over issues of this kind are overtly political. An abstract policy is one thing; a very public decision to do something which will mean thousands of job losses – perhaps in a part of the country already with high unemployment – is another. This is where economics and politics can come into conflict. Policy-makers at official level may be able to marshal powerful economic arguments in favour of disengagement – letting a company fail with all the consequences that would involve. The political gloss on such analyses may tip the balance in the opposite direction.

Another part of the answer lies in something rather more abstract and equally difficult to rationalise in strictly economic terms. The car industry is a good example. If car manufacturers cannot survive without large amounts of taxpayers' money, then they must be doing something wrong: they must be inefficient. In strictly economic terms they should be left to go bust, since other producers are already able to make cars more efficiently and cheaply. But besides the prospect of lost jobs there is the prospect of having to admit to large-scale industrial failure, which governments are reluctant to do. There may be occasions, it is argued, when an injection of cash will enable a company to get over temporary difficulty; there may also be occasions when so much public money has already been spent that one last instalment makes sense. But these are extremely difficult judgements for policy-makers. Experience has tended to show that, in most cases, such aid is throwing good money after bad, but politicians are naturally reluctant to take a decision which will impose painful economic adjustment on a sector or region.

But attitudes have changed. The Thatcher government was much more willing to see companies go to the wall rather than bail them out with public funds. There were occasions when business generally found economic conditions very difficult, such as in the recession of the early 1980s, when interest rates, inflation and the exchange rate were all very high (while demand was falling). The government stuck to its view that the market must operate as freely as possible, a view subsequently shared by both the Major and Blair governments. Policy-makers, while recognising that they may sometimes be the architects of corporate misfortune, no longer feel obliged, on the whole, to provide emergency help.

Inward investment

But if lame duck companies are no longer seen as legitimate recipients of public funds, policy-makers take a different view about using taxpayers' money to lure foreign companies to the UK. International investment flows are now many times larger than trade flows. International companies can now locate their manufacturing operations wherever in the world it is cheapest and most convenient for them to do so. Governments in many industrial (and developing) economies therefore compete to attract such companies, and will offer financial inducements to help tip the balance.

The UK has been uniquely successful in this: it gets about 23 per cent of total foreign direct investment in the EU, and about 40 per cent of all US direct investment in Europe. In 1997, the total stock of US foreign direct investment in the UK was £112 billion. Much inward investment needs no government encouragement: foreign companies are keen to own all or part of successful British companies, including an increasing number of financial institutions. But a variety of government and public agencies seek to encourage foreign manufacturers to base their operation in the UK, as this creates jobs and, in some cases, exports too.

Inward investment raises two issues for industrial policy and, more generally, for economic policy. The first is the issue of ownership. Until relatively recently there was strong popular and political resistance to the take-over of British companies by overseas concerns. There was a feeling that it was not appropriate for large companies to be foreign-owned. This was essentially an emotional response. Economic policy-makers tended to take a somewhat more hard-headed approach. Short of imposing restrictions on ownership, which would be hard to square with the prevailing belief in free markets, there is anyway little governments can do to prevent take-overs (provided that they do not conflict with competition laws – see below). Since in some cases, at least, the British company might not survive on its own in an increasingly global market, and the alternative – closure – would be worse. Moreover, British companies are themselves extremely acquisitive: British outward investment levels are also among the world's highest.

There are drawbacks to inward investment, however. The subsidiaries of foreign-owned companies usually remit the bulk of their profits to the overseas parent: this creates outward capital flows, in this case from the UK. And when a company is foreign-owned, the likelihood increases that the parent company will take decisions which are unpalatable for the UK. Only additional government funds stopped BMW switching Rover production out of the country.

These disadvantages have not stopped successive governments from trying hard to attract foreign companies to site manufacturing operations in the UK. At the end of the twentieth century, some of the most successful manufacturers in Britain were foreign. Nissan, Toyota and Honda all make cars in Britain. Sony, Samsung, Siemens, Bosch, Pfizer – the list is endless. But measuring the net benefit for the British economy of such investment involves some difficult calculations. All these companies receive a substantial package of grants and tax incentives when they set up plants in the UK. Some of these will come direct from central government and some from local authorities and regional investment agencies, whose job is to bring in foreign companies. Many factors affect a company's decision to invest in a particular country. But all parties acknowledge the importance of the financial inducements on offer: these can be critical because of the intense international competition for such investments.

Advocates of such inward investment argue that the effect of these companies on the British economy has been beneficial, not just in terms of the number of jobs created in one locality, and the consequent boost for the local economy, but also in terms of their influence on domestic manufacturing efficiency. These benefits, however, are impossible to quantify properly. Opponents, for example, criticise the effort put into attracting such operations because of the essentially low-skilled nature of the jobs being provided. The money spent in attracting them could, they argue, be more productively spent in other ways. In the end, the arguments tend to be emotional ones, since it is difficult for advocates and opponents of such investment to marshal figures in support of their particular view. But even those who favour the effort and public money expended on attracting companies to the UK question the wisdom of having different areas within the country competing against each other for the same investment, and sometimes bidding up the final cost in terms of financial inducements on offer.

Privatisation

If nationalisation was one of the hallmarks of the early post-war attempts at industrial policy, privatisation – its exact opposite – became one of the most distinguishing features of the late twentieth century. Begun in the early years of the Thatcher government and continued under the Major and Blair governments, privatisation became one of Thatcher's most successful and popular policies. It transformed the running of public utilities in the UK and at the same time hugely widened share ownership. And it has been replicated as a policy around the world: in other industrial countries and in what are known as the transition or emerging market economies.

The underlying principle is simple. The government has gradually sold off most of the assets which it previously 'owned' by issuing shares in them and transferring ownership to the new shareholders. In most cases the share sale was designed to encourage individual shareholders to buy shares, as well as the larger institutional shareholders (such as pension funds and unit trusts), which own the bulk of shares in the UK. Various inducements were used to attract individual shareholders, the most important being low prices for small share allocations, which usually guaranteed buyers the prospect of substantial returns. In some cases, the government retained what was known as a golden share – a share which gave it a veto power over certain transactions, such as sale of the company to a foreign owner. These special rights were rarely exercised and eventually abandoned in most cases. In the case of sales of nationalised industries which were also monopolies, state ownership was replaced by state regulation: independent regulators were appointed to ensure that the newly independent companies were not allowed to exploit their monopoly position.

During the 1980s and early 1990s, all the main public utilities – gas, electricity and water – which had been in public ownership for decades, were sold off, along with British Telecom, the steel and coal industries, and the rail network. A large range of companies which the government owned or part-owned, including Cable and Wireless and BP, were also moved fully into the private sector. Parts of the London Underground system and the Civil Aviation Authority were earmarked for sale when the Blair government took office. The rationale was that all these concerns could be more efficiently operated in the private sector, away from interference from government ministers and officials, and that more competition could be introduced.

But privatisation was a policy arrived at by accident. It was not a feature of the incoming Thatcher government's election manifesto in 1979. Decisions were taken relatively early on to offload some of the companies, such as Amersham International and the National Freight Corporation, which the government believed it was anomalous to own, but there was no initial plan to proceed with large-scale sales. That changed with the success of the initial sell-offs. There was a strong demand for shares, not least from individual investors, many of whom had never previously bought shares. Increasing the individual's stake in the economy was something which appealed to the government, and policy-makers now saw how this might be achieved.

At the same time, the constraints on the investment plans of the large state industries had become a serious problem. Macroeconomic policy, in particular the drive to cut government borrowing, was squeezing nationalised industries even tighter, just as the longstanding investment shortages began to pose serious problems for some of these industries. Moving them to the private sector would not only improve their management, but would also, policy-makers realised, free them from externally imposed and arbitrary investment constraints. The water industry, for example, needed to boost its investment programme significantly during the 1980s and 1990s in order to meet EU targets on water and sewage provision. Privatisation enabled it to do so. Privatisation also enabled the concept of competition to be introduced into state-run companies: plans were made to open up hitherto monopolistic markets in a bid to drive down the price to the consumer. By 1999 both the electricity and gas markets had been opened up in this way.

Ministers were also attracted by the prospect of using privatisation receipts to reduce the government's borrowing requirement. During the 1980s and early 1990s very large sums were raised from privatisation sales. But the treatment of these receipts was controversial. Although they were always clearly identified, the Treasury counted them as a reduction in the government's borrowing needs rather than as part of the financing of that borrowing requirement. There was much criticism of the fact that capital sales were in effect being used to finance current spending – another example of the blurring of the distinction between the two so common in public sector accounting (see Chapter 9).

Some privatisation exercises were politically controversial. The decisions to privatise the water industry and the rail network were politically controversial at the time and subsequently, in part because the newly sold off companies failed to meet performance expectations. There has also been considerable public disquiet about some of the high salaries earned by directors of privatised companies. But overall the policy has been widely judged successful. Privatised companies have responded well to competition. The regulatory structure put in place for the monopolistic industries (telecommunications, gas, electricity, water and rail) were largely successful, both in forcing prices down and in introducing real competition.

In spite of Labour's opposition to the privatisation policy when it was being carried out, the Blair government decided against reversing it and indeed announced plans for further sales. The British approach has also been adopted around the world. From 1983 onward, privatisation became a central feature of Conservative Party election policies, but its origins were accidental, and illustrate the extent to which economic policy tends to be reactive. Privatisation also shows the gains for policy-makers able to seize the moment.

Competition policy

At the beginning of this chapter we noted that industrial policy touches on some of the central issues of economic policy and management. It always has done. But by the end of the twentieth century some of these issues had become more urgent because of the difficulties faced by national policy-makers in an era of increasing globalisation. We have seen the pressure on governments to respond to the difficulties British companies often found themselves in – some coping with problems of their own making, others struggling with a more difficult, more competitive environment. Globalisation generally reminds policy-makers of their limitations. But the multinational nature of much economic activity makes competition policy a particularly sensitive issue.

Given the widespread belief in the virtues of competition and open markets, it may seem strange to think of a policy intended to regulate competition. But the US, the world's largest and most successful economy, has one of the toughest and oldest competition policies (or anti-trust policies as they are known there). Competition policy is designed to safeguard competition, to make sure no one company gets so big that it is able to distort the market, by pushing prices up or by forcing remaining competitors out. In the US, those policing the anti-trust laws have enormous powers, and they exercise it. At the turn of the century, Standard Oil, then the world's largest company, was broken up into several companies on anti-trust grounds. The same thing happened to AT&T in the 1980s. No one company is allowed to control more than a certain share of the market. Take-overs or mergers which come close to this figure must get clearance from the Federal Trade Commission.

In the UK, and in Europe, policy is more complicated. This is partly because competition policy in the EU is now controlled by the European Commission, which has tough but complex rules. The British government has its own rules, operated until 1999 by the Monopolies and Mergers Commission and since then by its successor, the Competition Commission. But the British attitude towards mergers and take-overs has long been ambivalent, partly because of the relatively small size of many British companies, especially compared with those in the US. British policy-makers tried not to make it more difficult for British companies to compete in world markets. Some mergers (such as those in the car industry in the 1960s) were actively encouraged. The British authorities were also reluctant to prevent mergers which they believed would strengthen the UK's industrial capacity. Increasingly, however, EU competition policy grew tougher, placing limits on the freedom of action of member states in this area.

Governments and growth

The ambivalence of policy-makers has been a recurring theme in this chapter. Industrial policy is an area of economic policy where it is difficult to separate emotional responses from reasoned argument. Policy-makers want to change the growth capacity of the national economy, but they do not really know how. We saw in Chapter 6 how governments have tried to improve the supply side of the economy by raising the level of skills, education and the flexibility of the work-force. Industrial policy is motivated by similar concerns. In the past it was often difficult for policy-makers to avoid the overwhelming temptation to interfere when they could see things going wrong; and to resist becoming involved in industry as a result of political pressure from workers or managers or owners. Yet most policy-makers would concede that it would be more sensible to create the right framework within which industry can thrive and then let it do so. The thrust of policy in the late twentieth century moved gradually towards acceptance of that view.

Conclusions

The sharp-eyed reader will have noticed by now that this has not been a comprehensive survey of economic policy, in the sense that it has not been possible to examine every aspect of policy. Little has been said, for example, about the split between central and local government responsibilities, or about supervision of the financial sector. A list of areas which the book has done no more than touch on could easily be compiled if one were so inclined. But that would be to miss the point. As I said at the beginning, this book's aim is not to provide an exhaustive study of the policy detail. That would not be feasible in such a short volume, and it would not anyway serve the purposes intended here. Instead, I have sought to provide the reader with an understanding of the context in which policy is made; the processes involved; and some of the principal issues with which policy-makers have to grapple.

Several points have become clear over the preceding chapters:

1 The linkages between the various strands of policy are intricate and complex. A policy decision in one area can have significant consequences in many other areas of policy – many of which can be unexpected and certainly unpredictable. One has only to look at the experience of the UK's membership of the ERM to appreciate this: as we saw, it had far-reaching implications for counter-inflationary policy; the exchange rate; and, ultimately, economic growth.
2 Policy-makers are often forced to make decisions in the dark. They cannot be sure of the consequences of what they decide, partly because of the difficulties of making accurate economic forecasts and partly because they usually have only an imprecise understanding of the status quo.
3 There is often a wide gap between desirability and feasibility. Policy-makers – especially politicians – may have very clear views

about what they want to achieve and how they want to achieve it. But in a democracy they may find it very difficult to persuade the electorate of their views – even popular governments find themselves backtracking on policy decisions in the face of popular opposition. Moreover, the electorate is not the only influential group to which policy-makers must pay heed: multinational corporations, foreign governments and the financial markets can all bring pressure to bear. And even if all these hurdles have been cleared, there are occasions when what looks possible turns out not to be because the realities of economic life are not as policy-makers had understood them.

4 Many economic policy decisions are ultimately political. There will be times when policy-makers choose a second-best option in one area of policy because they conclude it will improve their chances of a policy success elsewhere. Or they go down a particular policy route because they feel it is politically expedient: Margaret Thatcher's reluctant decision to join the ERM in 1990 is a clear example.

5 Economic policy cannot be made in a vacuum, nor can it be tried out in laboratory conditions. There will always be other factors to take into account when formulating policy, not all of them obvious at the time. And policy error – in formulation or execution – has to be accommodated. In real life, policy-makers get no second chances. If something does not work, they cannot go back to the drawing board and try again. They have to live with the consequences and try to find another way of achieving their policy objective.

A changing world

There have been huge changes in British economic policy in the last half century or so; indeed, there have been huge changes in the last twenty years. These reflect the speed at which the world itself has changed. The British economy is very different than it was just after the Second World War. Then the UK was heavily dependent on manufacturing – for output, growth and jobs. By the end of the twentieth century, the service sector had overtaken manufacturing, both in its share of GDP and in the number of people it employed. Work patterns are changing. More women are working and more people are working flexible hours. More people are working very long hours, and more are working part-time.

As we begin the third millennium, we are told that the pace of change is quickening, that the changes seen in the past fifty years are as nothing compared with what we can expect in the future. The information revolution is under way. A decade ago, almost no one had a mobile phone: today there are some twenty-four million of them in the UK. The Internet was virtually unknown five years ago. Now tens of millions of people around the world – including the UK – are connected and conducting an increasing part of their daily business through the net. It is impossible to predict what will happen next.

Yet some things have not changed as much as we might think. The UK is still an open economy: to a much greater extent than many others, it depends on overseas trade and on overseas investment – investment coming into Britain and investment made by British firms elsewhere in the world. What happens elsewhere has immediate and often direct repercussions on the UK and, inevitably, on British policy-making. It is not the business of this book to try to predict the future. But I know I am on safe ground when I say that the changes in the world economy now predicted by some can only increase the inter-dependence between the UK and the rest of the world.

I can also confidently predict that it will not make the task of the economic policy-maker any easier. The factors that make it difficult now will make it even more challenging in the future.

Further reading

Note: this is a suggested list of books for further reading, not a comprehensive bibliography.

B. W. E. Alford, *Britain in the world economy since 1880*, Longman, 1996

M. J. Artis, ed., *The UK economy*, Oxford University Press, 1996

M. J. Artis, N. Lee, eds, *The economics of the European Union*, Oxford University Press, 1994

A. B. Atkinson, *Incomes and the welfare state*, Cambridge University Press, 1995

Tony Benn, *The Benn diaries*, Arrow, 1995

W. Bonefeld, A. Brown, P. Burnham, *A Major crisis? The politics of economic policy in Britain in the 1990s*, Dartmouth, 1995

Roger Bootle, *The death of inflation*, Nicholas Brearley, 1997

Samuel Brittan, *Steering the economy*, Penguin, 1971

Kathleen Burke, Sir Alec Cairncross, *Goodbye Great Britain*, Yale University Press, 1992

Tony Buxton, Paul Chapman, Paul Temple, eds, *Britain's economic performance*, Routledge, 1994

Sir Alec Cairncross, *The Wilson years: a Treasury diary*, Historians' Press, 1997

Frances Cairncross, Sir Alec Cairncross, *The legacy of the golden age: the 1960s and their economic consequences*, Routledge, 1992

James Callaghan, *Time and chance*, Collins, 1987

John Campbell, *Edward Heath*, Pimlico, 1994

Bernard Connolly, *The rotten heart of Europe*, Faber & Faber, 1995

N. F. R. Crafts, N. W. C. Woodward, eds, *The British economy since 1945*, Oxford University Press, 1991

Edmund Dell, *A hard pounding*, Oxford, 1991

Edmund Dell, *The Chancellors*, HarperCollins, 1996

John Fforde, *The Bank of England and public policy*, Cambridge University Press, 1992

Denis Healey, *The time of my life*, Penguin, 1990

Edward Heath, *The course of my life*, Hodder & Stoughton, 1998

Peter Hennessy, *Never again*, Vintage, 1993
K. Holder, K. Matthews, J. Thompson, eds, *The UK economy today*, Manchester University Press, 1995
Sir Geoffrey Howe, *Conflict and loyalty*, Macmillan, 1995
Roy Jenkins, *A life at the centre*, Macmillan, 1994
Roy Jenkins, *The Chancellors*, Macmillan, 1998
Dennis Kavanagh, Anthony Seldon, eds, *The Major era*, Macmillan, 1994
William Keegan, *Mr Lawson's gamble*, Hodder & Stoughton, 1989
Paul Krugman, *Peddling prosperity*, Norton, 1994
Nigel Lawson, *The view from No.11*, Bantam, 1992
R. Layard, S. Nickell, R. Jackman, *Unemployment*, Oxford University Press, 1991
Angus Maddison, *Dynamic forces in capitalist development*, Oxford University Press, 1991
Angus Maddison, *Explaining the performance of nations*, Edward Elgar, 1995
Angus Maddison, *Monitoring the world economy 1820–1922*, OECD, 1995
K. O. Morgan, *Callaghan: a life*, Oxford University Press, 1997
Richard O'Brien, *Global financial integration: the end of geography?*, RIIA/Pinter, 1991
Ben Pimlott, *Harold Wilson*, HarperCollins, 1992
Philip Stephens, *Politics and the pound*, Macmillan, 1996
Michael Stewart, *Keynes and after*, Penguin, 1991
Susan Strange, *International economic relations of the western world, 1959–71*, RIIA/Oxford University Press, 1976
Susan Strange, *Casino capitalism*, Blackwell, 1986
Susan Strange, *Mad money*, Manchester University Press, 1998
Dennis Swann, *The single European market and beyond*, Routledge, 1991
Dennis Swann, *The economics of the common market*, Penguin, 1995
Margaret Thatcher, *The Downing St years*, HarperCollins, 1993
Helen Thompson, *The British Conservative government and the European exchange rate mechanism, 1979–94*, Pinter, 1996
Loukas Tsoukalis, *The new European economy*, Oxford University Press, 1993
Hugo Young, *This blessed plot*, Macmillan, 1998

Index

Note: a page number in *italics* indicates that the reference is to be found within a box.